The Complete

MARJORY FLEMING

The Journals, Letters & Verses of
MARJORY FLEMING
*in collotype facsimile from
the original manuscripts in the*
NATIONAL LIBRARY OF SCOTLAND
Edited by Arundell Esdaile
(525 copies only)
Cr. 4to.   42s. net

Sidgwick & Jackson, Ltd.

The Complete

MARJORY FLEMING

her Journals, Letters & Verses

transcribed & edited by
FRANK SIDGWICK

With a Portrait

London
Sidgwick & Jackson, Ltd.

First published 1934

PRINTED IN GREAT BRITAIN
BY R. & R. CLARK, LIMITED, EDINBURGH

PREFACE

THIS book, comprising the first complete transcript of all Marjory Fleming's manuscripts now known to be extant, owes its origin immediately to Mr. Arundell Esdaile's recent facsimile edition of the MSS., which he has carried out in the form outlined in his letter to *The Times* in May 1930: 'a complete facsimile without any transcript (still less any paraphrase) but with a bare minimum of biography, notes and illustrations'. Six months after that letter there appeared in the same columns the Rev. Dr. Archibald Fleming's letter (17th October 1930) announcing the presentation of Marjory's MSS. to the National Library of Scotland; and Mr. Esdaile thereupon obtained the permission of the Trustees to prepare his edition.

No doubt the ideal way to study Marjory's work is to visit the National Library of Scotland and peruse the originals: certainly the next best way is to read them in Mr. Esdaile's edition, where Marjory's own roundhand text is reproduced with the photographic verisimilitude of the collotype process. But Marjory's 'posthumous lovers' are of all classes and dwell in all corners of the earth; it does not fall to the lot of every one to visit Edinburgh (as Horace said of Corinth), and many others may covet but be unable to possess themselves of the book of facsimiles. I discovered, moreover, in the course of preparing the runways for the launch of Mr. Esdaile's edition, that on the one hand Dr. John Brown's *Pet Marjorie*, the source of so many people's knowledge of her work, has long been out of print, while on the other the only current edition, the late Mr. Macbean's, was derived not from the MSS. but from Brown's transcript of them.

Hence arose the idea of a fresh transcript and its rendering in typographical facsimile. A brief experiment convinced me that a line-for-line reproduction of Marjory's text, though in cold type, preserves much more of the quaint flavours and staccato rhythms of her own sentences than can emerge through the regimented lines and paragraphs of Mr. Macbean's sedate pages. For the same reason Marjory's errors, corrections, deletions and interlineations must be preserved, as well as the underlinings by which Isa Keith drew her pupil's attention to misspellings. This method of rendering a childish script, sometimes straggling and producing short lines of type (as on p. 68), sometimes closing up and producing long lines of type (as on p. 129), naturally lends the pages an appearance of irregularity, which could only be avoided by troublesome and expensive means.

This type-transcript acknowledges its derivation by following Mr. Esdaile's facsimiles page for page. The three Journals therefore appear in the chronological order at which he, after hesitation, arrived : it exactly reverses the order followed in Mr. Macbean's edition, but seems to me unchallengeable. I have prefaced each Journal with a brief statement of the evidence for date and place, and enlarged on the ' dating-points ' in the notes ; there are at least ten of them, and only two had been previously noticed.

As for criticism, I heartily endorse Mr. Esdaile's detestation of the ' fog of sentimentality ' in which Marjory's Victorian editors swathed her. Dr. John Brown certainly spread her fame far and wide ; but to-day we deprecate both the gushingness with which he describes 'the warm, rosy, little wifie' and the serene pedantry with which he edits her ' prattle' to suit his own taste. To others who turn away from Brown's *Pet Marjorie* with queasy sensations I would recommend a wholesome astringent in a passage from Mark Twain, who writes of her in language that would have shocked (I hope) Dr. Brown and (I fear) Isa Keith, but would (I think) have attracted Marjory herself by its force :

' She was made out of thunder-storms and sunshine, and not even her little perfunctory pieties and shop-made holinesses could squelch her spirits or put out her fires for long. Under pressure of a pestering sense of duty she heaves a shovelful of trade godliness into her journals every little while, but it does not offend, for none of it is her own ; it is all borrowed, it is a convention, a custom of her environment, it is the most innocent of hypocrisies ; and this tainted butter of hers soon gets to be as delicious to the reader as are the stunning and worldly sincer-ities she splatters around it every time her pen takes a fresh breath.'

Yet with however severe a brow an editor approaches Marjory, cheerfulness will keep breaking in, and I have been unable to push detachment to the point of referring to the eight-year-old author as Miss Fleming.

The text of Letter II, the original of which is missing, is reprinted from Macbean's edition by kind permission of *The Fifeshire Advertiser* Ltd., through Mr. Andrew T. Richardson. The original MSS. of Letters VI and VII are respectively owned by the Rev. Dr. Archibald Fleming and Dr. J. R. Hall Walker, who have kindly given me permission to reproduce them here. For various items of biblio- graphical and other information I am indebted to the expert knowledge of Mr. F. J. Harvey Darton, Mr. Michael Sadleir, and Dr. Geoffrey Keynes. Above all I am conscious of having tested almost to breaking-point a longstanding friendship by plying with innumerable questions Mr. A. Francis Steuart of Edinburgh, on whose extensive and peculiar researches into Scottish history and genealogies I have relied for many details.

F. S.

CONTENTS

Frontispiece

MARJORY FLEMING : after the water-colour sketch by
Isabella Keith preserved with the MSS. in the National
Library of Scotland.

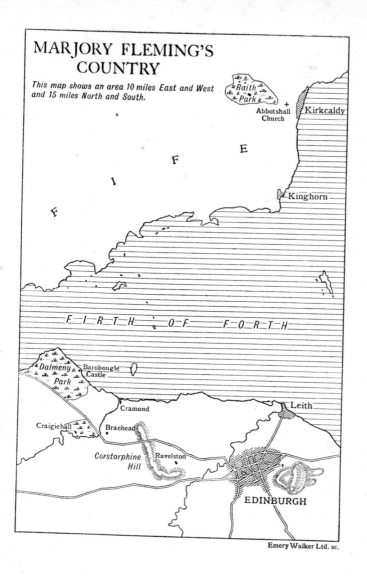

MARJORY FLEMING'S COUNTRY

This map shows an area 10 miles East and West and 15 miles North and South.

Raith Park

Abbotshall Church

Kirkcaldy

F I F E

Kinghorn

F—I—R—T—H— —O—F— —F—O—R—T—H

Dalmeny Park

Barnbougle Castle

Craigiehall

Braehead

Cramond

Leith

Corstorphine Hill

Ravelston

EDINBURGH

Emery Walker Ltd. sc.

INTRODUCTION

I.—Marjory

THOSE who require an introduction to the works of Marjory Fleming must first realise—and then continually bear in mind—the fact that, despite their world-wide reputation, they are the product of a little girl, an early-nineteenth-century Scottish girl, who died before she was nine years old. They consist of three 'journals', some verses and a few letters, all written in the last three years of her short life; in mere quantity, these literary remains, prose and verse, are approximately equivalent to the libretto of a Gilbert-and-Sullivan operetta.

She was born on the 15th of January 1803, third child and second daughter of James Fleming, accountant, of Kirkcaldy, Fife, and his wife Isabella. She came of good stock on both sides. Her father's forbears, Flemings of Perthshire, had fought at Killiecrankie and at Culloden. Her paternal uncle Thomas was, at the date of her birth, minister of Kirkcaldy Parish Church; later, of Lady Yester's in Edinburgh. Marjory's mother, born Rae, was the youngest daughter of an Edinburgh surgeon, sister to two other surgeons (John Rae became President of the Royal College of Surgeons, Edinburgh), sister-in-law to another doctor (William Keir), and, most importantly for Marjory, sister-in-law to William Keith of Ravelston. (The pedigree-table on p. xiv will make these relation-ships clear.) The Raes in their youth moved in the cultured circles of Edinburgh, and amongst their companions knew the young Walter Scott. Thus in heritage and environment Marjory was fortunately placed.

From their first page to the end, the Journals are full of 'Isabella'[1] and 'Isa', Marjory's devoted and worshipped cousin Keith, the paramount influence in her life and thought. The Journals, indeed,

[1] Marjory was surrounded with Isabellas: her mother, elder sister, cousin, and friend, Miss Craufurd, all bore the name.

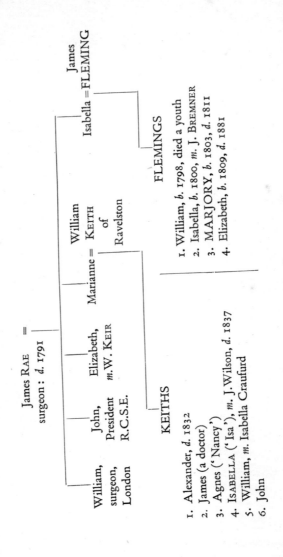

James Rae =
surgeon : d. 1791

William,
surgeon,
London

John,
President
R.C.S.E.

Elizabeth,
m. W. Keir

Marianne =
William
Keith
of
Ravelston

Isabella = FLEMING
James

KEITHS

1. Alexander, d. 1832
2. James (a doctor)
3. Agnes ('Nancy')
4. ISABELLA ('Isa'), m. J. Wilson, d. 1837
5. William, m. Isabella Craufurd
6. John

FLEMINGS

1. William, b. 1798, died a youth
2. Isabella, b. 1800, m. J. Bremner
3. MARJORY, b. 1803, d. 1811
4. Elizabeth, b. 1809, d. 1881

owe their origin to a visit that Isabella Keith, then about seventeen,[1] paid to her Kirkcaldy cousins, for this inaugurated an intimacy between herself and Marjory which resulted in Marjory's spending most of her sixth, seventh and eighth years away from her home, at Edinburgh, Ravelston or Braehead[2] (the home of the Houison-Craufurds), under the wing of her aunt, Marianne Keith, and under the immediate care and tuition of Isabella. *Journal I* at once informs the reader that 'Isabella teaches me everything I know', and the conclusion of the next page makes it clear that the daily record was not a purely spontaneous effort on the writer's part but a task imposed by the teacher, who subsequently under-lined the misspelt words for the benefit of her pupil. The com-pleted Journals Isa submitted to Marjory's family at Kirkcaldy,[3] in lieu, one may guess, both of the pupil's 'home letters' and of the teacher's terminal reports; but they were Isa's valued pro-perty which, after Marjory's death, she 'relinquished only to her Mother'.

In July 1811 Marjory returned home to Kirkcaldy. On 1st September she wrote (Letter V): 'we are surrounded with measles at present on every side'. In November she caught the disease, apparently recovered, but succumbed to its fatal sequel, then described as 'water in the head'.[4]

The Journals consist of three common 'copybooks', $7\frac{1}{2} \times 6$ inches, of plain paper watermarked 1802, 1808 and 1810, the pages ruled, for the young writer's guidance, almost throughout with double

[1] She was at least eleven years older than Marjory. The date of her birth does not appear to be recorded; enquiries have established only the fact that it was before 1792.

[2] In actual distance, Marjory was never much more than a dozen miles from her home: Isabella with 'a little glass' could see, from the southern shore of the Firth of Forth, Raith Tower hard by Kirkcaldy (Appx. B). See Map, p. xi.

[3] Appx. A.

[4] Dr. Geoffrey Keynes, kindly replying to a suggestion of mastoiditis, considers meningitis more probable as the cause of death. It is tragic to reflect that her mother's father and two brothers were eminent surgeons.

lines.[1]   Seventy-seven leaves (154 pages, of which 9 are blank) have survived ; *Journal III*, now nineteen leaves, certainly lacks at least two (4 pp.) at the beginning.   In all they contain some 9000 words of prose and 560 lines of verse.

This material, the basis of Marjory's unique reputation, came to light, like Samuel Pepys's Journals,[2] almost by accident and in extracts of gradually increasing amount.   The history of this piece-meal revelation is told below ; but as it has little to do with Marjory herself, setting forth only her posthumous legend, the reader, possessed of the foregoing details, and with a finger in the genealogical table and the map, may proceed direct to the Journals.   He may like to realise that the outer world, from which rumours reach Marjory's pages, was concerned with war : Trafalgar was fought in her infancy, and Sir John Moore died at Corunna in the year in which the Journals begin.

II.—HER MANUSCRIPTS AND EDITORS

With very little delay after Marjory's death, her manuscripts were returned to her mother by Isa Keith (whose letter, Appx. D, makes this clear) ; and for nearly half a century they remained unknown in the hands of her family.   Her father died about 1840, her mother ten years later, and her brother William died young in India.   Isa Keith married in 1824 James Wilson the zoologist (brother of ' Christopher North '), had two children, and died in 1837. Isabella Fleming married a Kirkcaldy merchant, J. Bremner, whose descendants alone carry on Marjory's branch of the family.   Elizabeth Fleming—the ' Baby ' mentioned by Marjory in Letter II—survived unmarried until 1881.

Marjory and her writings were first exploited in 1858 by H. B. Farnie, a London journalist and operatic librettist whose version of

---

[1] See p. 133.

[2] It is perhaps worth noting that both Marjory and Pepys called their daily tasks ' Journals ', which the modern world, to whom ' journal ' means nothing but ' newspaper ', tends to miscall ' Diaries '.

Les Cloches de Corneville is still in occasional use. He appears to have been wandering in and writing about Fifeshire, and must have been shown the Journals by one of the Flemings. His *Pet Marjorie : a Story of Child Life Fifty Years Ago,* first appeared in the *Fife Herald,* and was then republished as a sixpenny booklet, in a lithographed paper cover, with joint imprints of publishers in Edinburgh, Kirkcaldy and Cupar (1858). This *editio princeps* quotes about one-eighth of Marjory's prose and about a quarter of her verse. Farnie imposed on his subject the title and spelling ' Pet Marjorie ', under which she has laboured ever since ; but, *pace* Mr. Macbean's remark (in his fifth edition [1]) that Farnie in so naming her was ' following the family tradition ', there is no internal evidence to support either the ' Pet ' or the termination ' -ie '. Her own evidence and her family's prove that her name was Marjory, and that she was called familiarly Madgie, Maidie, and Muff or Muffy. But ' Pet Marjorie' is now carved on her (modern) tombstone in Abbotshall Churchyard at Kirkcaldy.

Five years later a rival expositor appeared in the field. In 1863 Dr. John Brown, M.D., of Edinburgh, contributed to the *North British Review* an article which was avowedly a review of Farnie's booklet (as it bore his title) but in fact a much more elaborate revelation of Marjory and her works. Brown acknowledges his indebtedness to ' her surviving sister' (Elizabeth) for the loan of the letters and Journals, a lock of her hair, and ' two pictures of her by her beloved Isabella ' ; and his quotations comprise twice as much of her prose as Farnie had given, and a hundred lines of her verse. Elizabeth Fleming also wrote to him the letter [2] which provides the sole direct evidence for Sir Walter Scott's friendship with Marjory. Out of this hint—unless he obtained other unrecorded evidence from the same source—Brown evolved the highly coloured opening to his essay, depicting Marjory and Scott as intimates, she reciting Shakespeare on his knee. Brown can hardly have risked publishing so circumstantial a story under Elizabeth Fleming's eye, unless she had

[1] This fifth edition in fact retains the spelling ' Marjorie ' in its title, but the text reverts to ' Marjory '.

[2] Appx. E.

supplied the material; yet neither Scott nor Marjory mention each other in their Journals, save for her single allusion to him as the author of her favourite poem 'Helvellyn' (p. 120). 'Sir Walter', Elizabeth Fleming writes,[1] 'was no relation of Marjory's': the connection is that he was her aunt's husband's first cousin's son. It is not inherently improbable that the two met, as Scott was undoubtedly a familiar visitor to his cousins the Keiths, and in his youth a friend of Marjory's mother.

Brown's review stimulated Farnie to produce a second edition[2] of his booklet, in the preface to which he acknowledges 'the kind and genial service rendered by the distinguished author of *Rab and his Friends*, who has so happily introduced it and its heroine to a wider audience', and admits to having made a 'somewhat free use' of Brown's fresh material: actually he conveys the whole of the Scott episode, as well as other quotations. Brown immediately retaliated by issuing '*Marjorie Fleming: a Sketch, being the paper entitled "Pet Marjorie: a story of child life fifty years ago"*', by John Brown, M.D., author of *Rab and his Friends*. Reprinted from the *North British Review*.' Though this is dated 1863,[3] Brown had certainly seen Farnie's second edition:

'The separate publication of this sketch has been forced upon me by the "somewhat free use" made of it in a second and thereby enlarged edition of the "little book" to which I owe my *introduction* to Marjorie Fleming—but nothing more;—a "use" so exceedingly free as to extend to almost everything.'

After this 'little act of conveyancing', as Brown further called it, Farnie's efforts ceased; and for forty years Brown's *Pet Marjorie* held the field alone, both in booklet form and as an item in the essays collected under the title *Horae Subsecivae*. Throughout many editions the essay remains substantially the same, but Brown later added to it a condensed and careless version of Marjory's letter to her mother.[4]

---

[1] Appx. E.
[2] Dated 1864 on the title-page, but the preface is dated 'December 1863', and the British Museum copy is stamped '22 Dec. '63'.
[3] The British Museum copy is stamped '23 Feb. '64'.
[4] Letter II, pp. 161-2.

At some time or another [1] he also took a complete copy of the Journals, remarkably accurate in some respects but not in all, which in due course descended to his son and became the basis of Macbean's edition. Facsimiles of four pages of this copy were reproduced by Macbean in his first edition (1904), but are absent from his latest (1928).

Meanwhile it was undoubtedly Dr. John Brown's essay that carried Marjory's fame round the world, evoked the famous tribute from Robert Louis Stevenson, made Swinburne imagine, in an elegy on Brown,

> ' Some happier isle in the Elysian sea
> Where Rab may lick the hand of Marjorie ',

and earned for her a niche as the youngest subject in the *Dictionary of National Biography*, Leslie Stephen himself carving the figure. It is, nevertheless, now possible to see that Brown was an untrustworthy editor ; and the fact that he took editorial liberties with Marjory's plain and legible roundhand cannot but create suspicion of his treatment of her history and traditions. When we find that, in printing Marjory's first letter (Letter I, p. 157) :

> ' My dear Isa,
>   I now sit down on my botom to answer. . . .'

Brown omits ' on my botom ', we may readily excuse him, remembering that it happened in 1863. (Farnie had naturally done the same, though he made it worse by professing to reproduce the letter ' word for word '.) But much less easily can we forgive Brown for his deliberate alterations of Marjory's text,[2] especially those in her two most famous poems on the Turkeys and the Charming Pug. These

---

[1] Macbean in his fifth edition (1928) prints for the first time a letter to Elizabeth Fleming, ' My Dear Friend ', from ' Yours Affectly., J. Brown ' : ' I am getting more and more taken up with Marjorie, and I think I would like to see the originals. I mean to put in as much more as I can, but I do wish you would write me a long letter, telling her little story in your own words. . . .' This Macbean dates as written in 1873. Was Brown contemplating a further enlargement of his essay, or is the date possibly misprinted for 1863 ?

[2] See notes on pp. 23, 24, 29, 54/5, 102, 147, 148/9.

must have been intentional editorial corrections, though no doubt Brown thought he was improving a rude text exactly as Bishop Percy thought he was improving the old ballads. It is only fair to repeat that Brown's copy of the Journals, so far as it can now be tested,[1] directly through Macbean's four facsimile pages or indirectly through Macbean's print from it, is on the whole painstaking and faithful.

In 1880, a year before her death, Elizabeth Fleming consigned Marjory's manuscripts and one of Isa Keith's portraits of the author to the custody of an old friend, the Very Rev. Dr. Macgregor, of St. Cuthbert's, Edinburgh, who duly respected her wishes that they should remain ' to a certain extent concealed from visitors'.[2] Dr. Macgregor held the manuscripts until his death in 1910.

In 1904 came the issue of Mr. Lachlan Macbean's *The Story of Pet Marjorie*, written and printed in Marjory's own environment at Kirkcaldy. Mr. Macbean provided for the first time an almost complete text of all Marjory's writings, and accompanied them with illustrations of ' her portraits, books, and other relics' placed at his disposal by Captain Bremner, the son of her sister Isabella ; he also diligently collected traditions from 'ladies who had known her [Marjory's] mother and sister'. He was thus enabled to compile a valuable and in many respects still indispensable book, the success of which proved that Marjory's ever-growing public were eager for every scrap of information concerning her.[3] Unfortunately, the one most essential ingredient—Marjory's own original MSS.—he was unable to secure ; consequently for his text he had to fall back upon Brown's copy, which was lent to him by the Doctor's son—' a copy so carefully made', says Mr. Macbean, ' that it was almost a *facsimile*, for it reproduced all the child's errancies and erasures, the vagaries of her spelling and punctuation, and even Isa Keith's rebukes'. The original MSS. meanwhile lay hid in Dr. Macgregor's safe in

[1] Brown's transcript cannot now be traced.

[2] Cf. the Rev. Dr. Archibald Fleming's address at the opening of Marjory's birthplace as a museum for her relics, etc., in 1914 (Macbean, 5th ed., 1928, p. 129).

[3] Editions have appeared since in 1905, 1914 and 1928 : an American edition, nominally the third, was published in 1904.

Edinburgh ; it was not until 1914, by which time they had passed into the Rev. Dr. Archibald Fleming's custody in London, that Mr. Macbean, then preparing his fourth edition, could announce their survival. But even in the latest edition (1928) of his book, his text of the Journals remains substantially what it was in the first.

Now that it is possible to compare Macbean's text with the original MSS., it is also possible to testify to the high degree of accuracy achieved by this copy of a copy : nevertheless a number of errors have crept in, at first or second hand, between what Marjory wrote and what Mr. Macbean printed from Brown's copy. In the absence of the latter, a full collation is impossible, even were it worth while ; but an examination of the four pages of Brown's transcript reproduced by Mr. Macbean suffices to show that Brown made mistakes which Macbean copied, and other mistakes which Macbean correctly emended by guess, and also that Macbean made mistakes of his own.[1] Further, he rendered the Journals into paragraphs that were not always indicated in Brown's copy, which in its turn arranged the original into paragraphs not indicated by Marjory. Macbean or Brown placed the three Journals in an order which it is impossible to reconcile with such dates as can be elicited from Marjory's few allusions to contemporary events.

To sum up, Marjory's three editors have given to the world the following amounts of her writings :

Editor			PROSE (words)	VERSE (lines)
FARNIE (1st edition)	.	.	1150	150
BROWN	.	.	.	2380	100
MACBEAN	.	.	.	8900	560

It only remains to add that the manuscripts, and the portrait by Isa Keith reproduced in this book, remained in the charge of the Rev. Dr. Archibald Fleming, Minister of St. Columba's, Pont Street, London—' a namesake, though not a relative, of the child '— for nearly twenty years, seen by only a few. In 1930, with the

[1] See notes on pp. 5-6 and 96-100.

approval of the heirs of the widow of Dr. Macgregor, Dr. Fleming handed them over to the Trustees of the National Library of Scotland.[1] Thus they are permanently housed in the 'conspicuous town' of Edinburgh, within a few miles of the places where Marjory wrote them.

[1] See his letter to *The Times*, 17th October 1930.

NOTE ON THE TRANSCRIPT

THE original copybooks containing the Journals are uniform in size of page, but the number of double lines ruled by (or for) Marjory varies from a minimum of 10 (p. 69) to a maximum of 19 (p. 152). The lines at the head and foot of the printed pages may be taken as indicating the tops and bottoms of the MS. pages; but it was not considered worth while to space the printed lines out to fill each page in the manner of the MS.

Where the pages of the MS. have been shortened by cutting or tearing, the fact is recorded (e.g. pp. 17/18, 19/20). Where Marjory has omitted to write anything between her ruled lines, I have noted it as, e.g.,

'[one line blank]'

It would have been useless to try to note all Marjory's failures to cross her t's and dot her i's; and in one or two instances of apparent errors apparently corrected, I have given her the benefit of the doubt.

I cannot hope to have avoided all mistakes; but it is open to any one who suspects a reading to refer to the book of facsimiles, and check or improve upon my interpretation.

F. S.

JOURNAL I

Spring and early Summer, 1810

NEAR the top margin of the opening page (p. 3) is a scrawled "My jur", and another similar attempt, upside-down, at the head of p. 4. These support the indications that this is Marjory's first Journal.

Dating-points are provided by her allusions to the Exhibition opened in April 1810 (on pp. 6 and 14) and (on p. 18) to the King's birthday; 1810 was George III's jubilee year, and June 4th his birthday.

The Journal begins at Edinburgh, where Marjory is visiting the Keiths at 1 North Charlotte Street; Isabella Keith, her cousin and teacher, is introduced at once. Marjory's father comes over from Kirkcaldy to see her (p. 11). A two-day visit to Braehead, owned by the Houison-Craufurds, intimate friends of the Keiths, follows (p. 17); from p. 22 to the end Marjory appears to remain "in rurel filisity" at Braehead.

Many people are hanged for Highway

robbery Housebreking Murder &c &c

Isabella teaches me everything I know

and I am much indebted to her she is learn

5 ⁓en witty & sensible.—I can but make a

poor reward for the servises she has

done me if I can give her any but

I doubt it.—repent & be wise saith the

preacher before it be to late.—Regency

10 b^onnets are become very fashionable

of late & every _∧body gets them save poor me

but if I had one it would not become

me.—A Mirtal is a beautifull plant

& so is a Geramem & nettel Geramem

Climbing is a talent which the bear

excels in and so does monkeys apes &

baboons.—I have been washing my

dools cloths today & I like it very much

5 people who have a good Concience is alwa*ys*

happy but those who have a bad one is al-

-ways unhappy & discontented

There is a dog that yels continualy

& I pity him to the bottom of my heart

10 indeed I do. Tales of fashionable life ar*e*

very good storys Isabella campels me

to sit down & not to rise till this page

is done but it is very near finished

only one line to write

Yesterday the thunder roared & now

and then flashes of lightning was seen

but today their is no such thing & far

from it, for it is very warm sunny

5 & mild.—The Monkey gets as many vi-

-sitors as I or my cousins.—Nobody

can be happy that has guilt on his

mind.   Grandeur & Magnificence

makes one Proud & Insolent

10 peevish & petish & these make us mise-

-rable & unhappy besides people

will hate us & abhor us and dispise us

We should get the better of our pas

-sion & not let then get the bet

-ter of us

Osians poems are most beautiful.—I am very

strong & robust & not of the delicate sex

nor of the fair but of the deficent in look

People who are deficient in looks can make up

5 for it by virtue.—I am very fond of the

Arabin nights entertainments & wish to

read the tales of the Genie. Silver & Gould is ve[ry]

presous.—I am fair as the sun & beautiful as

the moon. I hear many people speak

10 about the Exebition and I long very much

to behold it but I have to little mony

to pay the expence.—Queen streat is a

very gay one & so is Princes streat

for all the lads & lases besides bucks & beg-

⸮ars parade there.—Tomsons him to the sea

sons is most eligant & most beautifull & so is

young Celidon & his Emelia but is melancho

⸮ly & distresing poor man his fate was

5 a dismale he was an unhappy lover

A Mr Burn writs a beautifull song on

a M Cunhaming whose wife desar

ted hin truly it is a most beautifull one

I like to read the Fabulous ~~his~~historys

10 about the historys of Robin Dickey

flapsay & Peccay & it is very amuse

ing for some were good birds and

others bad but Peccay was the most

dutifull & obedient to her parents

15   [one line blank]

I went into Isabellas bed to make her smile

like the Genius Demedicus the statute in an-

-cient Grece but she fell asleep in my very fa^{ce}

at which my anger broke forth so that

5 I awoke her from a very comfortable nap

all was now hushed up but agan my an-

-ger burst forth a^t her biding me get up

I have read in the history of Scotland how

Murry the regent was shot ~~was~~ by Hamilton

10 of Bothwellhaugh but Murry used Hamil

-tons wife very ill & drove her quite mad

but Hamilton should have left Murrys

punishment to God Almighty for revenge

is a very very bad thing & aught not

15 to be done

Many people are so sinful as to steal &

murder but they have punishment either

from God or men in this world or the next

In the New whole duty of men, that says

5 that family prayer should be well aten

-ded to.   I should like to see a play very much

for I never saw one in all my life &

dont believe I ever shall but I hope I

can be content without going to one

10 I con be quite happy without my desire

be granted People should set others

an exampal of doing good

for every body is happy that do-

eth good

Nancys and Isabellas uncle has got Musical

Glases & the sound of them is exceeding

sweet.—The poetical works of tomas Grey are

most beautifull espacially one the death

5 of a favourite Cat who was drowned in

a Tub of fishes.—When books are funy &

amuseing I am very fond of them such

as the araiban nights entertaintents

& the Tales of the Castal &c &c.—Every

10 body should be unasuming & not a-

suming.—We should regard vir-

tue but not vice for that leads us to

distriction & makes us unhappy all

our life

Some days ago Isabella had a tereable fit of the

toothake and she walked with a long nightshift

at dead of night like a gost and $_\wedge^{I}$ thought she

was one she prayed for, tired natures sweet

5 restorer bamy sleep but did not get it

a ghostly figure she was indeed enought to ma^{ke}

a saint tremble it made me quever & shake

from top to toe but I soon got the beetter

of it & next morning I quite forgot it

10 Superstition is a very very mean thing

& should be dispised & shuned

An adreß to my ~~ft~~ father when he came

to Edinburgh My father from Kercaldy ca^{me}

but not to plunder or to game

15 Gameing he shuns I am very surre

For he has a hart that is very pure

Honest & well behaved is he

And busy as a little Bee

I am very fond of some parts of Tomsons

seasons.—I like loud Mirement & laugh

5 ~ter.—I love to walk in lonely solitude

& leave the bustel of the nosey town

behind me & while I look on noth~

~ing but what strikes the eye ~~bu~~ with

sights of bliß & then I think my~

10 self tronsported far beyond

the reach of the wicked sons of

men where their is nothing but strife^(fe)

& envying pilefring & murder

where neither contentment

15 nor retirement dweels ~~not~~

but there dwels drunken^(ness)

Beautious Isabella say

How long at breahead will you stay

O for a week or not so long

Then weel desart the busy throng

5 Ah can you see me sorrow so

And drop a hint that you must go

I thought you had a better hart

Then make me with my dear friends ^part

But now I see that you have not

10 And that you mock my dreadful lot

My health is always bad and sore

And you have hurt it a deal more

The reason I write this poem is because

I am going to Breahead only two

15 days

I like to here my own sex praised but

not the other.—The vision is most beau

-tiful Breahead is a beautiful place

& on a charming situation

5 I should like to see the Exibition very

much & still more so the theater

I am reading the misteris of udolpho

with Isabella & am much interes-

ted with them I have got some of

10 Popes works by hart & like them

very much.   the days are very long

and very light just now which is

very pleasant to me & I darsay to

every body

I should like to go and see the curosities

in Londen but I should be a little affr^aid

of the robbers For that country is greatly

infested with them at Edinburgh their

5 is not so many of them

Their is a very nice book called The

Monk & the Vinedreser written by a

lady but I do not know her name

It is true that

10 Death the rightious love to see

But from it doth the wicked flee

I am sure they fly as fast as their legs

can carry them My cousin John

has a beautiful musaim & he has got

15 many nice curiosities

Macbeth is a fearful play. I pityed

Mary Queen of Scots when the

people held a standard on which

was painted the dead King and

5 *his son kneeling and uttering*

these words judge & revenge my

cause O Lord. I should not liked to

have been her but I think it was very

wrong in the people to mock their

10 *sovereign & queen I have seen*

her picture & think her most

Beautiful & Angelick Elisbeth

behaved very crually to poor

poor Mary

Today O today I am going to Brea

-head but alas my pleasure will

be soon damped for I must com^e

home in too days but I wish to stay

5 too months or more for I am very

fond of the country and could

stay at Breahead all my life

There the wind houles to the waves

dashing roar but I would not we^ep

10 my woes there upon any ac-

-count

[the bottom of the page is torn off]

To days ago was the Kings Birthday

And to his healh we sung a lay

Poor man his healh is very bad

And he is often very mad

5 He was a very comely lad

Since death took his girl from his si-*ght*

He to her grave doth walk at night

His son the grand grard *of york* Duke

I'm sure he eateth plenty pork

10 For I do hear that he is fat

But I am not so sure of that

_____

[the bottom of the page is torn off]

[top of page torn off]

Of summer I am very fond

And love to baith into a pond

The look of sunshine dies away

And will not let me out to play

5 I love the morning sun to see

That makes me from the house to flee

I love the morning sun to spy

Glittring through the casements eye

The rays of light are very sweet

10 And puts away our taste of meat

[top of page torn off]

My lover Isa walks with me

And then we sing a prity glee

My lover I am sure shes not

But we are content with our lot

5 Often I have heard people say

In the right path I love to stray

But wickedneß I cannot bear

To walk with it I will not dare

The trees do wave their lofty heads while

10 the winds stupenduous breath

wafts the scattered leaves afar off

besides the declifities of the rocks

leaves that once was green and beauti-

full now withered and all wed away

5 scatering their remains on the footpath

and highroads &c &c

The balmy brease comes down from heaven

And makes us like for to be liveing

But when we that if we died

10 No pleasure there would be denied

There happineß doth always reign

And there we feel not a bit pain

In the morning the first thing I see

is most beautiful trees spreading their

15 luxurant branches between the Horison &

me

There is a thing I love to see

That is our monkey catch a flee

With lo^oks that shews that he is prou^d

He gathers round him such a crowd

5 But if we scold ˄^him he will grin

And up he . . ll jump and make a din

I love to see the morning sun that

rises so long before the moon the

moon that casts her silver light whe^n

10 the Horison sinks beneath the cloud^s

and scateres its light on the surface

of the earth ; Here at Brea⸜

head I enjoy rurel filisity to per⸜

fection, content, retirement

rurel quiet frienship books, all these

dweel here but I am not sure of ease

and alternate labour useful life

I love in Isas bed to lie

5 O such a joy & luxury

The botton of the bed I sleep

And with great care I myself keep

Oft I embrace her feet of lillys

But she has goton all the pillies

10 Her neck I never can embrace

But I do hug her feet in place

But I am sure I am contented

And of my follies am repented

[one line blank]

I am sure I'd rather be

In a smal bed at liberty

poor Emily

& am much interested in the fate of poor

top.   I am reading the Mysteries of udolpho 5

I could not have done had I slept at the

Arabin nights entertainments which

well continualy at work reading the
&

nial figiting and kicking but I was very

turbed her repose at night by contu- 10

the bed becase Isabella says that I dis-

At Breakhead I lay at the foot of

In a smalll at liberty

I am sure I'd rather be

On Jeßy Watsons Elopement

Run of is Jeßy Watson fair

Her eyes do sparkel she's good hair

But Mrs Leath you shal now be

5 Now and for all Etenity

Such merry spirits I do hate

But now its over and to late

For to retract such vows you cant

And you must now love your galant

10 But I am sure you will repent

And your poor hart will then relant

Your poor poor father will repine

And so would I if you were mine

But now be good for this time past

15 And let this folly be your last

Oar hills & dales fair Phillip strayes

And he doth walk through all the ways

He and myselfe are lovers true

We can feal pangs as well as you

5 Those that feal pangs are not so few

We walked apon the distand hills

And often goes into the mills

        h
Very soft & wite his cheeks

His hair is fair & grey his breaks

10 His teath is like the daisy fair

The only fault is on his hair

I am beginning to be jealous

And feel a small degree of malice

That kindeles in my bosom fair

And fills my hart with great despair

Ah man you said you once loved m^e

But from your promises you flee

The sun is seen glimering through the

5 trees whose spreading foilage allows only a

slight tinge to be seen it is a Beautiful sight

In the dining room & drawing at Breahea^d

The walls are hung with the pictures of there^fie

ancestors both men and weomen

10 The hedges are green the trees are green

& every thing bears a pleasure to the

eye when we look on them

Thre^e is some beautiful trees behind the house &

before the house which makes it very

I have been a Naughty Girl

I have been a Naughty Girl

The lofty trees their heads do shake

When the wind blows, a noise they make

5 When they are cut a crash you hear

That fills your very soul with fear

Tis like the thunders loudest roar

You would not like to hear much more

It makes the earth begin to quake

           its mity
10 And all ~~And all its~~ pillers shake

The viabration of the sound

Will I am sure you quit(e) confound

It makes the mountains to resound

[one line blank]

Dedicated to M^{rs} H Crawfurd by the author MF

Three Turkeys fair their last have breathed

And now this worled for ever leaved

Their Father & their Mother too

5 Will sigh & weep as well as you

Mourning for th~~eir~~ osprings fair

Whom they did nurse with tender care

Indeed the rats their bones have cranched

To eternity are they launched

10 T~~here~~ graceful form & pretty eyes

Their fellow pows did not despise

A direful death indeed they had

that would put any parent mad

But she was more then usual calm

15 Sse did not give a singel dam

She is as gentel as a lamb

Here ends this melancholy lay

Farewell poor Turkeys I must say

Tis, eve, the wind is very boisterous the

sea must be very tempestious while the

waves montain high dashes in the ships side

5 overturnes it & launches the crew into eternity

I love to see the mornings light

That glitters through the trees so bright

Its splended rays indeeds full sweet

And takes away our tast of meat

10 I love to see the moon shine bright

It is a very nobel sight

Its worth to sit up all the night

But I am going to my tea

And what I'v said is not a lee

15   [one line blank]

[P]oor Williams gone to Giffords fair

To see the things that are seen there

I'm sure he will be much amused

For to such things he is not used

5 There lads and & laßes he will see

                       well

Dreßed as gay as can ~~sure~~ be

I have been often at a fair & am alwys

very much interested & amused with it there

are always a great concorse of people at it

10 Here I pas my life in rurel filicity festivi-

ty & pleasure I saunter about the woods & forests

Breahead is ~~is~~ far far sweeter then

Edinburgh or any other place

Every thing is beautiful some colour is red

15 others green & white &c &c but the Trees

& hedges are the most beautiful for they are

of the most pretty green I ever beheld in

all my life

Goodneß of hart gentelneß & meekneß makes
one beloved & respected by those who are
acquainted with them but pride insolence
and bad hartedneß is always hated
5 and despised it is better to follow after
the first then after the last for the first
is good and the last is bad

Of sauntering about the doors I am
very fond especialy when it is a
10 fine & sunny day. I am very fond
of Spring Summer & Autun but I am
not so fond of winter for then it is
cold & dreeiry

Isabella says that when we pray we should

pray fervently & not rattel over a praye^r

when our thoughts are wandering but to collect

our thoughts for that we are kneeling at the

5 footstool of our Lord & creator who we

ought to respect honour & obey with due

revirance & fear he created us & he may

take away our blisings if he pleaes

He showers down bliβings on our heads

10 when we least deserve them & forgives

our sins & forgetfulneβ of him our

Lord & creator who saved us from mesi-

ry & eternal damnation, from un-

questionable fire & brimston he sav

15 -ed us

When cold as clay when cold as ice

To get into a bed tis nice

It is a nice thing for to creep

But not to dose away & sleep

5 Into a bed where Isa lies

And to my questions she replies

Corrects my faults improves my mind

And teels me of the faults she find^d

But she is soun asleep sometimes

10 For that I have not got good ~~thy~~ ^{rimes}

But when awake I her teize mu^{ch}

And she doth squall at every touch

Then Isa reads in bed alone

And reads the fasts by good Nelson

15 Then I get up to say my prayers

To get my porridge & go down stairs

JOURNAL II

Summer, 1810

AT the head of p. 37 is written in Isa Keith's hand the word 'Braehead'. With a visit or visits to Ravelston, the Keiths' own house, Marjory stays at Braehead till the end of the Journal.

A clear dating-point is given by Isa Keith's entry on p. 40, where she has fortunately not obliterated the date 'Thursday July 12th', which must refer to 1810. Minor natural indications of the season are perhaps to be seen in the thunderstorm (p. 58) and the gooseberries that made Marjory's 'teath watter' (p. 77). At the end (p. 91) it is 'frosty'.

The people comprise her hostess at Braehead, Mrs. Craufurd, and her daughters Margaret and Isabella (who subsequently married William Keith); Mr. George Craigie of Craigie-hall hard by Braehead; Mr. Philip 'Caddle' (doubtless a Cadell of Cramond); Mr. Bonner, who preached, and his wife and daughter; the Keiths themselves; and some doubtful Johns and Williams who are sometimes Keiths and sometimes apparently 'sarvents'.

It may perhaps be suspected that the cause of the leaf pp. 73-74 lacking an inch and a half of its full length at the top was the 'dreadful passion' it records.

The Day of my existence

here has been delightful &

enchantinting. On Satur-

day I expected no leß than

5 three well made Bucks the

names of whom is here ad-
          are
vertised Mr. Geo Crakey

and Wm Keith and

J^n Keith, the first is the

10 funniest of every one of

them Mr. Crakey &

I walked to Crakyhall han[d]

by hand in Innocence and

matitation sweet thinking
<u>ed</u>
on the kind love which

5 flows in our tenderhearted

mind which is overflows

<u>re</u>
ing with majestick pleasu

nobody was ever so polite

to me in the hole state
<u>w</u>
10 of my existence.

Mr Craky you must

know is a great Buck &

pretty goodlooking

[one line blank]

I am at Ravelston

enjoying natures fresh air

5 *the birds are sin^ging*

sweetly the calf doth

frisk and play and

nature shows her glorious

face. the sun shines

10 *through the trees, it is de-*

lightful

Wednesday

[followed by 4 lines in Isa Keith's hand deleted]

Thursday July 12th

[followed by 5 lines in the same hand deleted]

5 *I confeß that I have been*

more like a little young

Devil then a creature for

        a

when Isabella went up

the stairs to teach me reli-

10 *gion and my multi-*

plication and to be good

and all my other leßons

I stamped with my feet

and threw my new hat

which she made on the

ground and was sulky an^d

5 was dreadfuly paßionate

but she never whiped me

but gently said Marjory^p

go into another room and

think what a great crime

10 n you are committing

~~and~~ letting your temper

git the better of you
e

but I went so sulkely that
i
the Devil got the better of me

but she never never whip[s]

me so that I thinke I would

5 be the better of it and the

next time that I behave

ill I think she should do it

for she never does it but she

is very indulgent to me but

10 I am very ungratefll to

Tuesday 4 . . Wednesday
hir

To Day I have been very

ungrateful and bad and

diſsobedient Isabella gave

me my writing I wrote

5 so ill that she took it

away and locted it up
       $\overline{k}$

in her desk where I

stood trying to open

[the bottom of the page is cut away]

it till she made me come

and read my bible

but I was in a bad honour
                    um
and red it so Careleßly
       a
5 and ill that she took

it from me and her

blood ran cold but she

never punished me

she is as gental as a lamb.

10 to me an ungrateful girl

_____

[the bottom of the page is cut away]

Isabella has given me praise

for checking my temper for I

was sulkey when she was
                even

kneeling an hole hourr teachin
                              g

5 me to write

[one line blank]

Yesterday I behave extreme
                           ly

ill in Gods most holy church

for I would never attand my-

10 self nor let Isabella attand

which was a great crime for

she often often tells me that when

to or three are geathered to-

od
gether Gis in the midst of

them and it was the very

same Divel that tempted

5 Job that tempted me I am

sure but he resisted satan

though he had boils and

many many other mis-

fortunes which I have es-

10 caped.——

I am now going to tell you

ched
about the horible and wret

plaege that my multiplication

gives me you cant concieve it—

the most Devilish thing is 8 times 8

& 7 times 7 it is what nature itselfe

5 cant endure

[the rest of the page is cut away]

I have a delight^{fu}l pleasure in

view which is the thoughts of go-

ing to Braehead where I will

walk to Craky-hall wich puts

5

me In mind

[the rest of the page is cut away]

that I walked to that delightfull

place with ~~that~~ a delightfull ~~place~~

young man beloved by all his

[blot] friends and espacialy by

5 me his lovereß but I must not

talk any longer about him ~~any~~

~~longer~~ for Isa said it is not

proper for to speak of gentalm an

but I will never forget him

10 I hope that at 12 or 13 years old

I will be as learned as Miß Isa

and Nancy Keith for many

girls have not the advan-

am

tage I have and I very very

glad that satan has not ge-

ven me boils and many other

o

5 Misfortunes, in the hly bible these

words are written that the

t

Devel goes abou like a roaring

lyon in search of his pray

but the lord lets us escape from

10 him but we sometimes do

not strive with this au-

full spirit

p

To Day I bronunced a

word which should never

come out of a ladys lips it was

that I caled John a Impu⸗
l

Isabella
dent Bitch and afterwards told

tttt me that I should never say

5 it even in joke but she kindly

forgave me because I said

tha I would not do it again

t
I will tell you wha I think

made me in so bad a homo⸗

10 ur is I got 1 or 2 cups of that

bad bad sina tea to Day

[one line blank]

Last night I behaved extre⸗

mely ill and threw my

work in the stairs and

would not pick it up ~~it~~

which was very wrong

indeed ; and all that

5 William could do I would

not go out of the room

till he himself _{put me out} I _{ed} ∧ and roar

like a bull and would

not go to bed though

10 Isabella bid me go

which was very wrong in

‑deed to her when she takes

so much pains with me when

she would like best to be walk-

-ing but she thinks it her du

-ty

5 As this is Sunday I must be-

gin to write serious thoughts

as Isabella bids me.   I am

thinking how I should Impro^ve

the many talents I have.

10 I am very sory I have

threwn them away it is

shoking to think of it when

~~have~~ ^not many have half

the instruction I have ~~the~~

because Isabella teaches

me to or three hours every

day in reading and

writing and arethmatick

5 and many other things

and religion into the bar

gan . On sunday she

teaches me to be virtuo^us

[one line blank]

10 Ravelston is a fine pla^ce

because I got balm win^e

and many other dain^ties

and extremely pleasan^t
^(it is)

to me by the company of swine

geese cocks &c and they are the de-

light of my heart.

I was at a race to Day &

5 liked it very much but we miβed

one of the starts which was very

provoaking indeed but I can

-not help it so I must not com

-plain lord Mongumorys gaine

10 horse gained it but I am clat-

tering so I will turn the subject

to another think ;—but no I

must git my spelling first

I acknowledge that this page is

15 far from being well written [torn]

[the bottom line is torn away]

Isabella teaches me my

leßons from ten till two every

day and I wonder she is

not tired to death with me

5 *for my part I would*

be quite Impatient if I

had a child to teach.

[one line blank]

It was a dreadfull thing

10 *that Haman was hanged on a*
   the ll
   gatows which he had pre

⁃pared for Mordica to hang

him & his ten sons thereon

[the bottom of the page is torn]

& it was very wrong & crua ^l

to hang his sons because they

did not commit the crime

but then Jesus was not then

5 come to teach us to be Mer-

-cifull ;,

Yesterday I behaved excee ^{dingly}

ill & what is Worse of

all is when Isabella told me

10 not to let my temper get

the better of me but I did

not mind her & sinned

away which was very nauty^{gh} ;

[one line blank]

Yesterday then thunder bolts

roled Mightiy^l oer the hils

5 it was very Majestick, but

to Day there has been no

thunder, but I will speak

about another thing ; .

[one line blank]

10 Yesterday I am very

glad to say a young

Cocker came to our house

to stay, it is very beautifu^{llt}

& it is named Crakey

it was Isabella that na^med

him & white & black is

its coualer but all the wh^ite

5   will come of is not that

wonderfull ;,

This is Saturday, & I

am very glad of it, be-

cause I have play

10 half of the Day, & I get

mony^e too, but alas I

owe Isabella 4 pence,

for I am finned 2 pence

whenever I bite my n^ails

Isa is teaching me

to make Simecolings nots
^{m}

of interrgations peorids & com
^{i}

-moes &^{c} ;

5 As this is Sunday

I will Meditate uppo
^{n}

Senciable & Religious

subjects first I should

be very thankful that

10 I am not a begger

as many are ~~I have~~

& ;.

I get my poetry now

out of grey & I thin^k

it beautiful & Majes-

tick but I am sorry

5 to say that I ~~le~~ thi^nk

it is very Difficult to get

by heart but we mus^t

bear it well ;

    I ~~think~~ Hope that Isa

10 -bella will have the good

-neß to teach me

Geografie Mathematicks

& Fractions &c. ;

The Scythians tribe

lives very corsly for a

Gluton Introdused

to Arsaces the Captain

5 of the Armey, 1 man

who Dreßed hair &

another man who was

a good cook but Araces

said that he would

10 keep 1 for brushing his

horses tail, & the other

to fead his pigs ;

Dear Isa is very in-

-dulgent to me, for whic^h

usage I am sorrow^y to

say, that I am alway^es

5 dog ^in something or other

ill, which is very nau-

gh ty, is it not, ;

   It is Malancholy

to think, that I hav^e

10 so many talents, &

many there are that

have not had the atten-

tion paid to them that

I have, & yet they

contrive to *be* better *a* then

5 me ;   Mrs Craford

has a dog & I believ^e

it is as beautifull as

any in good Old

England, I am sure ;

10 & she had 5 pups but

they are all drowned

but 1 ;

Now am I quite

happy . for I am going

tomorrow to a delightfull

place, Breahead by name,

belonging to Mrs Crra-

5 ford, where their is ducks
          re are
cocks hens bublyjocks 2 dogs
        &
2 cats swine. & which is
              k
delightful ; I thing
          c
it is shoking to think

10 that the dog & cat

should bear them &

they are drowned after
all

I would rather have

a man dog then a

a
women dog because they

do not bear like women

5 dogs, it is a hard case

c
it is shoking ;—

I came here as

I thought to enjoy na

⁄tures delightful breath

10 it is sweeter than

a fial of rose Oil

but Alas my hopes

are dißopointed, it is al-

ways spitring but then

I often get a blink

& than I am hap-

5 py

    Every Morn I

awake before Isa &

Oh I wish to be up

& out with the turkies

10 but I must take

care of Isa who

when aslipe is as

beautifull as Vineß

& Jupiter in the

skies ;

To Day I af-

fronted myself be-

fore Miß Margret

5 & Miß Isa Cra

-ford Mrs Craford

& Miß Kermical

which was very

nauty but I

10 hope that there

will be no more

evel in all my

Journal ;

~~To Day~~

To Day is Saturday

& I sauntered

about the woulds

5 & by the burn sid^e

& dirtied myself_e

which puts me in

mind of a song my

mother conp^o_sed it was

10 that she was out &

dirtied herself which

is like me ;

I am very sory

to say that I for-

5 got God that is

to say I forgot

to pray today &

Isabella told me

that I should

10 be thankful that

he did not forget me

if he did O what would

become of me if I was

in danger & God

not friends with me

5 I must go to un-

quenchiable fire & if

I was tempted to sin how

could I resist it I

will never do it again

10 no no not if I can help

it ;

    I am going to tell

you of a malancholy

story A young Turkie

of 2 or 3 month Old

would you believe it

the father broak its

leg & he kiled another

5 I think he should

be transported or

hanged ;

    Will the sarvent

has buried the Turkie

10 & put a tomeston &

written this is in memory

of the young Turke

[The page lacks 1½ inches at the top]

[one line blank]

I am going to tell you

that in all my life I

never behaved so ill for

5 when Isa bid me go out

of the room I would not

go & when Isa came to

the room I threw my

book at her in a dreadful

10 paßion & she did not lick

[The page lacks 1½ inches at the top]

me but said go into

room & pray & I

did it I will never

do it again I hope

5 *that I will never*

afront Isa for she

said that shs was

never so afronted in

her life but I hope

10 *it will nevr happen*

again

~~Oh to-day I am af~~

We expect Nancy

tomorrow I am hap-

py she is coming but

5 I would be still hap

      had

per if I behaved better

but I will be better ;

[one line blank]

I got a young

10 bird & I have tamed

it & it hopes on my

finger.   Alas I have

promised it to Miß

Bonner & the cage

is here & little

Dickey is in it ;

5 How O how shal

I recieve Nancy

after behaving so ill.

I tremble at it, it is

dreadful to think of

10 it, it is ;

I am going to turn

over a new life &

am going to be a very

good girl & be obedient

to Isa Keith,

here there is planty of

5 goosberys which makes

my teath watter ;

Yesterday there was campony

M^r & Mrs Bonner

& Mr Philip Caddle

who
10 paid no little attention

to me he took my hand

and led me down

stairs & shok my
^o

hand cordialy,

   A sarvant

5 tried to piosen

   mistreß & 2 3 child

   -ren, what a dread

   ful concience she

   must have ;

10   [one line blank]

[one line blank]

Isabella is by far too in-

dulgent to me & even the

Miß Crafords say that

5 they wonder at her patience

with me & it is indeed true

for my temper is a bad

one

_____

[The bottom of the page is cut away]

My religion is greatly

falling off because I

dont pray with so much

attention when I am say

5 ing my prayers & my

charecter is lost a-mong

the Breahead people I hope

I will be religious agoin

but as for reganing my

10 charecter I despare

_____

[The bottom of the page is cut away]

for it,

[one line blank]

Isa bids me give you

a note of the sarmon

5 *preached by M^r*

Bonner it was that we
sould o̱f̱e̱r ourselves to

God morning & evening

& then we will be happy

10 *with God if we are good*

[two lines blank]

At Breahead there is

a number of pictures

& some have monstrous

large wigs ;

every body just now

5 hates me & I deserve

it for I dont behave

well ;

[one line blank]

I will never again trust in

10 my own pow~~e~~r. for I see

that I cannot be good with⸗

⸗out Gods aßistence, I will

trust in my selfe & it

Isas health will be

quite ruined by

me it will indeed;

[one line blank]

5 I can never repay

Isabella for what

she has done but by

good behave-our.

[one line blank]

10 If I am good I will

be ∧ but if I am
  happy

bad I will be un-

happy

Isa has giving me

advice which is that

when I feal Satan

begining to tempt me

5 that I flea from

him & he would

flea from me.

　　　[one line blank]

John is gone

10 to Queensferry

to meat ser~~man~~ ^{vent}

Willman ; It is far ⁱ

better to behave well

then ill ;

[one line blank]

Let me give you

5 a note of the sar

mon it is that

if we are determ^{ined}

to be good & try

to be so that will^{we}

10 always succeed

for God when he

seas that ~~when~~

we are trying will

aßist us

[one line blank]

5 Many people say

~~that~~ that it is diffic^{ult}

to be good but it

is they will not try

to do it ;

10   [one line blank]

The best way to be

good is to pray to God

to give us aßistence &

if he gives us his aßistenc^e

I can say that I will

be good & we sould^h never

5 mind punishmen^t if it is

to do us good & it is better

to bare punishment if

it is to save us from brim

ston & fire ;— We are

10 reading a book abou^t

a man went ^who into

a house & he saw

a sack & he went &

look into it & he saw

a dead body in it
Marjory must write no more journal till she writes better

5 *Communications*

Communictions Commu-

nictions Communications

Communications Com-

munications Communication

                                                      i-
10 *Comunications Commun-*

cations Comunications

Communications.

Expectations Forwardneß ß

Expectations Forwardneß s

Expectations Forwardneß

Expectations Forwardneß

5 *Expectations Forwardneß s*

Expectations Forwardneß ß ß s

Expectations Forwardneß ß s s

Expectations Forwardneß ß ß s

Expectations Forwardneß ß s

10 *Expectations Forwardneß s*

Expectations Forwardneß

Expectations Forwordneß

Expectation Forwardneß

I know that if I try truly

to be good God will healp me

to be so & with his hep̶e alone
l

can we behave well indeed

5 *it is true & every body will*

see so ;

Nancy is too indulgent

& Isa I could not find
as to

one like her though I was

10 *to search the ∧ indeed peo-*
world

ple must say that, or

they will be false peo-

ple but I do not think

they will be so

m m m m m m m m

u u u u u u u u u u u

n n n n n n n n n

m m m n n m m,

5 This is Thursday & it was

frosty but the sun shins

in all its beauty it is very

romantick inded ;—

Isabella & Miß Isabella

10 Craford walks to Baron

bugal & jump with filisity

over wals & fences ;—

Life is indeed p^r asious to thos^e

who are good because they

15 are hapy & good indeed.

Remorse is the worst thing

to bear & I am afraid that

I will fall a marter to it

when I am going to

5 ~~I~~ Kerkaldy & to my

poor mother, again I

will tell you why ~~I k~~

~~so~~ it is that I have thrown

away many advantages

10 that athers have not tharefore I

I think I will fall a

victom to remorse ;—

There is four You

treas & Is sa caled 1

15 of them Lot & his wife

JOURNAL III

Spring, 1811

THIS Journal is paged, apparently by Marjory herself; p. 95 is labelled ' 5 ', p. 96 with a deleted ' 6 ', the fatal page 97 is un‐ numbered, p. 98 is ' 6 ', and thenceforward consecutively to p. 130, which is ' 38 '. It is clear that two leaves, pp. 1‐4, are lost at the beginning.

The locality seems to be mostly Edinburgh, as there is a distinct atmosphere of city life about several allusions; but about pp. 118‐119 she may have paid a visit to the country, Ravelston or Braehead.

The dating‐points indicate the spring of 1811 with complete certainty (see notes on pp. 95, 100, 109, 110, 123, and perhaps 105). The allusions to the weather suggest that a ' very mild winter ' (p. 104) was followed by cold and frost ' and plenty of ice ' (p. 113); towards the end a night ' was very cold but this morning is very warm ' (p. 126).

not be happy at the death of our fel

-low creatures, for they love life like us

love your neighbour & and he will ^love you

Bountifullneß and Mercifulneß

5 are always rewarded, Isabella has

admi^ra ble patience in teaching me mu

sick and resignation in perfection

In my travels I met with a

handsome lad named Charles

10 Balfour Esg^e, and from him I

[g]ot ofers of marage. offers of ma
x   x

[rria]ge did I say ? nay plainly

d me.—Goodneß does not belong

but badneß dishonour befals
x

wickedneß but not virtue, no

disgrace befals virtue, perciverence
                      x

overcomes almost all difficulties

no I am rong in saying almost
          x

5 I should say always, ~~as it is so~~

~~perciverence is a virtue & gl~~

my Cosin says pacience is a
     x   x

cristain virtue, which is true ;—
x

fortitude is of use in time of dis⸜

10 treß, & indeed it is always of

use ; many people have su[

in mesery & have not ~~m~~[
    x

~~ny~~ had fortitude ~~&~~[

~~were able~~ to suppreß there[

Careleß

Marjory

The *Divil* is *curced* & all his

works.—Tis a fine book New⸝

ton on the *profecies* ; [deletion]

[deletion] anther book of poems

5 comes near the bible ;—The Divel

always grins at the sight

of the bibles ; bibles did I say ? nay

at the word virtue, I should

like to learn Astronomy & Ge

10 ography ;—Miss Potune is very

fat she pretends to be very

learned she says she saw a

stone that dropt from the

skies, but she is a good christian

An annibabtist is a thing I

am not a member of :—I am

~~Pispliccan~~ a Pisplikan just

5 now & a Prisbeteren at Ker⸗

caldy my native town which

    o
thugh dirty is clein in the

country ;—sentiment is what

      i   i
I am not acquanted wth

10 [th]ough I wish it & should

    c
[li]ke to pratise it I wish I

[h]ad a great great deal

[o]f gratitude in my heart

[&] in all my body ;—The

English have great power ov⸝

er the franch ; Ah me perad⸝

⸝venture, at this moment some

noble Colnel at this moment

5 sinks to the ground without

breath ;—& in convulsive pangs

dies ; it is a melancoly consideration

Love I think is in the fasion for

every body is marring there

10 is a new novel published nam⸝

ed selfcontroul a very goo[d]

maxam forsooth Yesterday

a marrade ˄ named M^r

John Balfour Esg[e] offered

to kiß me, & offered to marry

me though the man was es-

pused, & his wife was prsent, &

5 said he must ask her per

-mision but he did not I

think he was ashamed or con-

founded before 3 gentelman

M[r] Jobson & two Mr Kings

10 Isabella teaches me to read my

bible & tells me to be good and

say my prayers, and every

thing that is nesary for a

good carecter and a good con

15 -science.——

Ephibol on my dear love Isabella

Here lies sweet Isabell in bed

With a nightcap on her head

Her skin is soft her face is fair

5 Aad she has very pretty hair

She and I in bed lies nice

And undisturbed by rats and mice

She is disgusted with Mr Wurgan

though he plays upon the organ

10 A not of ribans on her head

Her cheak is tinged with concious red

Her head it rests upon a pilly

And she is not so very silly

Her nails are neat her teath are white

15 her eyes are ~~white~~ very bright

In a conspicuos town she lives

And to the poor her money gives

Here ends sweet Isabellas story

And may it be much to her glory

All this is true and a full discrip-

5 tion.—In the love novels all

the heroins are very des-

-perate Isabella will not

alow me to speak about lovers

& heroins & tiβ too refined for

10 my taste a lodestone is a cu

-rous thing indeed it is true

Heroick love doth win disgra^{ce}
this
is my maxium & I will

follow it for ever &

Miss Egwards tails are very

good, particu*r*lay some that

are very much adopted

for youth as Lazy Law

5 ⸒rance & Tarelton False

Key &c &c.—Persons of the

parlement house are as

I think caled Advoca*te*kes

Mr Cay & Mr Crakey

10 has that honour, This

has been a very mild

winter,

Mr Banestors Budjet is tonight

& I hope it will be a good one.—

A great many authors have expreßed

themselfes too sentimentaly I am stu-

5 dying what I like, musick, Rih^ces

Wealth & Honour are to be desired

I have seen the Wild Beasts & they

are excelent particularly the

Lion & hunting Tiger the Ela𝑝

10 phant Bolted & unbolted a

door & such like wonders

but of all the birds I admired

the Pelecan of the Wilderneß

My Aunts birds grow every

15 day more healthy

The Mercandile Afares

are in a perilious situ-

-ation, sickneß & a delicate

frame I have not &

5 I do not know what

it is but Ah me perhaps

I shall have it, Grandure

reagns in London & in

Edinburgh there are a great

10 many balls & routs but

none here.—The childish

deses distempers are very

frequent just now

Tomson is a beautifull author &

Pope but nothing is like Shakepear

of which I have a little knlege ~~of~~

An unfortunate death James the

5 5 had for he died of greif.——

Macbeth is a pretty composition but

an awful one Macbeth is so bad

and wicked, but Lady Macbeth is so

hardened in guilt she does not

10 mind her sins & faults ~~ha~~

The Newgate Calender is very

instructive, Amusing, & shews us

the nesesity of doing good & not evil

Sorrow is a thing that sadines

15 the heart & makes one grave

sad & melancoly which dis

treses ~~his~~ relations & friends,

The weather is very mild

& serene & not like winter

A sailor called here to say

5 farewell, it must be dread-

-full to leave his native country

where he might get a wife

or perhaps me, for I love
him   i
~~very~~ very much & wth

10 all my heart, but O I

forgot Isabella forbid me to

speak about love.—A great

many bals & routs are geven

this winter & the last winter

15 too,—Many people think

beuty is better then virtue [torn]

[torn] one of our beauties just

now, Isabella is always readng &

writing in her room, & does not

5 come down for long & I wish every

body would follow her example

& be as good as pious & virtious as

ds

she is & they would get husban

soon enough, love is a very

10 papithatick thing as well as

troubelsom & tiresome but O

Isabella forbid me to speak a⸗

⸗about it.—General Grame

ch

has defeted the Franch the Fran

5 prisoners have made a tumbling

[torn] *and my cosin says it is very*

neat I heard that they ma[de night]

⁓caps of there blankets and bows to

make them smart and shewy

5 *My cosins are sober and well behave*^{d}

and very gentele and meak.—I

study writing & counting & deferent

accomplishments James Macary is to be

trasported^{n} for murder in the flow

10 *er of his youth O paßion is a terible*

thing for it leads people from sin to

sin at last it gets so far as to come

to greater crimes then we thought we

could comit and it must be

dreadfull to leave his native country
and his friends and to be so disgraced
and affronted.—The Spectator is a
very good book as well as an instruc-
5 -tive one Mr James and Mr John Da-
vidson are gone to that capital town
called London.—Two of the Balfours
dined here yesterdy and Chareles
played on the flute with Isabella
10 and they are both very handsone
but John has the pleasest expreßion
        an
of them all but he is not instrumental which
is a great loß indeed because it would af-
ford him amusement and diversion.—
15 Thre are a great quantity of books
        e

selling off just now.—I am come to poor
Mary Queen of Scots history which Isa
-bella explains to me and by that I un
-derstand it all or else I would not

5 Expostulations of all kind are very
frivolous Isabella thinks this nonsense
so I will say no more about Expos-
-tulations.—The Birds do chirp
the Lambs do leap and Nature is

10 clothed with the garments of green
yellow, and white, purple, and
red, Many people who have money squander it all away but
to do my cousins credit they do not

15 do so or behave so improperly
indeed they are not spendthrifts

or persons of that sort.   Good are re-
                    the

-warded in this wrld & the next as
            o

well as the comfort of there own cons-

-ciences, love rightousneß & hate ~~excel~~

5 evel and vice.—There is a book thats

is caled the Newgate Calender that

contains all the Murders,—all

the Murders I say, nay all Thefts

& Forgeries that ever ∧ commited.
                         were

10 & fills one with horror & consternation

Bredheade is a sweet place & in

a charming situation beside wood
                               s

& riveluts.—The weather is very cold

& frosty & plenty of ice on the grou
                                  nd

15 and on the watter Love your

enemy as your friend and not as

your foe this is a very windy stor-

-my day and looks as if it was

going to snow or rain but it is

5 only my opinion which is

not always corect.—I am reading

some noveletts and one call-

ed the Pidgeon is an excelent

one and a charming one—

10 I think the price of a pine-

apple is yery dear for I here

it is a whole bright goulden

geinie

that might have sustained a

poor family a whole week and more

perhaps,—Let them who $\overset{are}{temted}$ to do

wrong consider what they are

5 about and turrn away filled

with horror dread and affright

There is an old Proverb which $\overset{s}{say}$

a tile in time saves nine $\overset{h}{wich}$

is very true indeed.—Tawny

10 Rachel and the Cottage cook

are very good excelent books

and so are all the cheap

Repository books indeed

[one line blank]

Isabella is gone a tour to

Melrose Abbey and I

think she will be much

pleased with it & I hear

5 it is a very fine old build-

-ing indeed.—In the

Novellettes by Augustus Von

Kot zebue I have paid par

-ticular attention to one called

10 the Pidgeon because it is a nice

and a good story

The Mr Balfours are gone

far far away & I will

not so much as see or

hear of them anny more

5 but I will never for-

-get them never never

I am overpowered with the warm

-neß of the day & the warm

-neß of the fir^e & it is altoge-

10 -ther insufferable though

there is a good deal of wind

Exodus & Genesis are two

very good books as all the

bible is ~~& shall be~~ I am

sure of it indeed I like

5 *the old testament better*

then the new but the new

is far more instructive

then the old.—The hedges

are spruting like chicks

10 *from the eggs when they*

are newly hatched

or as the vulgar says clack-

-ed.—I pretended to write to

a lord Yesterday named

Lord Roseberry about kill-

5 ing crows & rooks that

inhabit his castle or estate

but we should excuse my

Lord for his foolishneß

for as people think I

10 think Too for people think he is

a little derangeed

My addreß to Isabella on her

return, Dear Isabella you are

a true lover of nature thou lay-

-est down thy head like the

5 meak mountain lamb

who draws its last sob by the side

of its dam, taken fom hill

Villean a poem by Walter

Scott & a most beautifull

10 one it is indeed this addreß

I composed myself & no-

-body aßisted me I am sure

I get acquanted with boys & girls

almost every day.—wickedneß

and vice makes one miserable &

unhappy as well as a concousneß

of guilt on our mind.—Doctor

5 Swifts works are very funny

& amusing & I get some by hart.—

Vanity is a great folly & some⁄

⁄times leads to a great sin disimu⁄

⁄lation I think is worse. This wa[s]

10 a bad day but now is a ~~bad~~ good one. Selfe⁄

⁄denial is a good thing and a vir⁄

tue.—Sᵗ Paul was remakable for his

releigion and piety he was in a grea

t

many periels & dangers

Many people that are pret‑

ty are very vain and conceated
     _d_
men praise and amire her, &

some finds their heart ake because

5 of her asks her to marry him

and dies if she refuses him but

is overpowered with joy if she
     _n_
consets to marry him

Wallflor grows very well I

10 think so at least.——Moreheads

Sermons are I hear much

praised but I never read

Sermons of any kind but

I read Novelettes and my

bible for I never forget it and

it would be a sin to forget it or my

prayers either of them

A g

5 on   [This portion

E   torn away]

        [? the foun]dation of

the barracks and we will per-

-haps be saccrifised to death and

10 the grave but soulders are in

serch for them & peradvenu^re

they will be found I sencerly

wish so

The Earl of Bucan says

we should take care of our

charector & our health poor

5   [Three lines torn away]

⸌tue, thou are what people

like O virtue !—Meat is

          dear
very nowadays.—People

                        n
10   *should not be proud or*

              n
saucy or vain for vani

ty is a sin

All the King James died me-
sirable deaths one of grfe, another
murdered, but Lord Darnlys
was the most cruel

5 Mary Queen of Scots was a prisoner
in Lochleven Castle.—The Casawary
is an curious bird & so is the Gigantick
Crane & the Pelican of the Wilderneß
whose mouth holds a bucket of fish & wa-

10 ter.—Fighting is what ladies is not gua
lyfied for they would not make a good
figure in battle or in a dual Alas we fe-
males are of little use to our country
& to our friends, I remember to have

15 read about a lady who dreßed

herselfe in mans cloths to fight for her

father, woman are not half so brave

as her, but it is only a story out of Mo-

thers Gooses Fary tales so I do not give

5 it cridit, that is to say I do not belive

the truth of it but it matters little

or nothing.—Last night it was

very cold but this morning is

        is an
very warm it extrordinary

10 change.—The history of all the

Malcontents that exer was hang-

ed is very amusing I have

read some of of these larned

men but they got there reward

15 in due form

Isabella this morning taught me

some Franch words one of which

is bon suar the interpretation

is good morning.—I like sermons

5 better then lectures.—Joy depends

on thou O virtue !.—Tom Jones &

Greys Elegey in a contry Church

yard are both excelent & much

spoke of by both sex particularly

10 by the men.   Personal charms

are as nothing if the hart is

not good & virtuous ;—A per⸗

son may be pretty & not good

& dutiful to her parents

Mary Queen of Scots confedrats or

friens w̲a̲s̲ defeated by M̲u̲r̲y̲s̲ &
d

his aßociat̲s̲ & thought she was safe
they

in the castle when she effected

5 her escape, by a young boy

named G̲o̲rge D̲u̲glas ;—

People who steal & murder

bring eternal damnation

in the next world upon

10 them, as well as unhappineß
selves

in this world.—Adam & Eve

dißibayed God.   The scarlet

f̲e̲f̲e̲r̲ is like a plague just now.

God is the creator of us all and we should serve

honour and obey him.—Isabella has often told

me that, if people do not chek their paßion

when they are young it will grow worse

5 and worse when they are old so that nobody

will love them or obey then.—Isabella is grei-

ved when I behave ill but when I behave

well she kißes and careses me and she

kißed me today because I behaved well.—God is

10 kind and indulgent to us which we do

not deserve for we are sinful

creaturs & do not deserve to be so

kindly treated but god does not do

so.—Though we pray in publick that

5 should not hinder us fron private

prayer.—If any mans wife marry

another man when her husband

is yet alive   [a line

deleted]   every body will hate her

5 & she shall be the object of there

deristion & there disgust

     i

The wcked are envious of the good &

       mind

just & in there ~~own~~ plot his distruction

but the lord does not leave him unpu-

10 -nished for if he is not punished in this

world he will be punished in the next

& a most terrible punishment

         ted

it will be.—Macary is not yet transpor

it must be a dreadful thing transportation.—God Almighty knows every

thing that we do or say & he can kill you

in a moment.—Bishop Sanaford excels

Mr James in preaching.—Lying is the

5 high road to theft & murder King John is

a beautiful play & so is King Rich-

ard the 3 I never saw a play acted in

my life.—Any body that does not do

well are very very misarable &

10 unhappy & not contented

[four lines blank]

POEMS APPENDED TO JOURNAL I

THE MS. book containing Journal I and these poems consists of 30 leaves, the Journal occupying the first 16 (our pp. 3-34), the poems (including 8 blank pages, occurring between our pp. 153 and 154) occupying the last 14 leaves.

The only date is Marjory's signature at the end, 'Kirkaldy July 19'. As her return home must be assigned to 1811, Mr. Esdaile suggests that this book, after the completion of Journal I at p. 34, was devoted to verses only, and another volume begun as a Journal.

It may be noted in support of this theory that of the 20 pages on which poems are written, 7 are ruled with single lines only, suggesting an advance in the art of writing ; all the rest of Marjory's MSS., Journals and letters alike, are written between double ruled lines.

The Life of Mary Queen of Scots by M.F.

[one line blank]

Poor Mary Queen of Scots was born

With all the graces which adorn

Her birthday is so very late

5 That I do now forget the date

Her education was in france

There she did learn to sing & dance

There she was married to the dauphin

But soon he was laid in a coffin

10 Then she at once from France retired

Where she had been so much admired

Farewell dear france she cried at last

While a desparing look she cast

The nobels came to meet there Quee

Whom they before had never seen

They never saw a face so fair

For there is no such beauties there

That with her they could compair

5 *She was a Roman Catholic strong*

Nor did she think that it was wro^{ng}

But they her faith could not well bear

And to upbraid her they would dare

Ther was a man that was quite good

10 *To preach against her faith he would*

His name was John Knox a reformer

Of Mary he was a great scorner

Her nation was so very feirce

                    could
That they your very hart peirce

15 *In love she fell & deap it was*

Lord Darnly was the very cause

A nobels son a handsome lad

by some queer way or other had

Got quite the better of her hart

5 With him she always talked apart

Silly he was but very fair

A greater buck was not found there

He was quite tall & slender too

And he could dance as well as you

10 Soon was the nupsials done & ore

Of it there was said nothing more

They lived togeather for a while

And happineß did there time beguile

Mary was charmed with a player

             a   great

5 Of whom she took great ∧ care

He fed upon the finest fair

He was her greatest favourite

Him she caresed with all her might

She gave him food she gave him wine

5 When he was gone she would repine

The King heard this with anger sore

This is not all there is much more

For he did murder the poor player

Of whom she took so great a care

10 In agony she heaved a sigh

For on the King she did relie

Bad hatered at length foud a way

It was a little more then play

An awful day at last arived

15 Which was the last that he survived

For she went to a masqurade

But for that thing he dearly paid

For her *in* absence what was done

The thing would not I'm sure give fun

5 The house in which the King did lie

I cannot think without a sigh

Was blowen up at too next day

The King was killed I'm sorry to say

Some degree of suspicion fell

10 On the mighty Earl of Bothwell

And of the Queen they did *think* too

That of that thing she quite well knew

For they do think that mary was

Of Darnlys death the very cause

But he was guiltleß of the crime

But it was only for that time

Mary went to meet her son

That thing did not give her much fun

5 For Bothwell under some pretence

And with a great deal of expence

Marched to a town there found the Queen

He was quite glad when she was seen

He then disperced her slender train

10 That did not give her any pain

His castle of Dunbar she went

It was just there that she was sent

Poor Mary did not shew much terror

great
I must say this is an error

15 This opportunity they catched

For there they did wish to be mached

To Edinburgh the Queen was brought

He was quite glad that she was caught

The castle was then in his power

His temper was quite bad & sowr

5 There she was lodged in the castle

Which was as bad near as the bastile

He was then married to the Queen

Of whom he did not care a pin

The nobles formed a conspiracy

10 On poor Bothwell & poor Mary

Kirkaldy of grange & some more

His name I did not tell before

The nobles soldiars were quite brave

And they there masters lives would sav*e*

15 Poor Bothwells friends were not the same

And spread a small degree of faim *but*

For their poor master they forsook

But in their base flight he pertook

For he said to the Queen, adieu

Those that behave so are but few

5 The King said to the Queen farewell

For his poor soldiers nearly fell

After Bothwell went away

In a humour not like play

She gave herselfe up with much ease

10 And she did try them all to plea se

The soldiars behaved very bad

It would indeed have put me ma d

For when she turned her eyes so bri ght

She always saw a dreadful sight

15 ~~Darnlys picture with her son~~

Darnlys Picture with her poor son

That did not give her any fun

Judge and revenge my cause cried he

This mary could not bear to see

5 Covered with dust droping a tear

A spectical she did appear

To break her marrage she would not

Though it would happy make her lot

This her bad nobles would not bear

10 Though she was then so very fair

To Lochleven was she then carried

She would not say she was not married

At last from prison she got away

She got from prison I do say

5 All her great arts she had employed

And the succeß she had enjoyed

Her keepers brother gained she had

He was a very fine young lad

At last she hinted that she would

5 Make him her husband if she could

On Sunday night the second of may

She did escape that very day

At supper when his brother sat

I have not got a rhyme for that

10 And all the family had retired

His cleverneß I much admired

One of this friends stole of the keys

To let her out when she did please

Let out poor Mary & her maid

15 Indeed she got from him much aid

But for that thing his brother pad

She got to the boat which was prepair ed

Nobody but george for her cared
did
There she meet her friends on shore

Who had been there some time before

At Setons house she sat some time

5 There she got good bread & good wine

She then got up & rode away
at
Full of gre mirth & full of play

To Hamilon she come at last

For she did galop very fast

10 Then she her followers all prepaired
t
And fealy to their Queen they sweared
a
They marched aginst the regent who

Could perhaps fight as well as you

Mary meanwhile was on a hill

15 Where she did stand up quite stock still

The regent Murry ganed them all

And every one of hers did fall

L

She then did mount again to ride

For in her friends she couldn't confide

She flew to England for protection

For Elisbeth was her connection
            ᵃ

5 Elisbeth was quite croß & sour

She wished poor Mary in her power

Elisbeth said she would her keep

And in her kingdom she might sleep

But to a prison she was sent

10 Elisbeths hart did not relent

Full ninteen years & mayhap more

Her legs became quite stif & sore

At last she heard she was to die

And that her soul would mount the
                                sky

15 She was qite overjoyed at this
         ᵘ

She thought it was her greates bliß
                              ᵗ

The hour of death at last drew nigh

When she did mount the scaffold high

Upon the block she laid her head

She was as calm as if in bed

5 One of the men her head did hold

And then her head was of I'm told

There ends all Queen Elisbeths foes

And those who at her bend their bows

Elisbeth was a croß old maid

10 Now when her youth began to fade

Her temper was worce then before

And people did not her adore

But Mary was much loved by all

Both by the great and by the small

15 But hark her soul to heaven did rise

And I do think she gained a prise

For I do think she would not go

Into the awfull place below

There is a thing that I must tell

Elisbeth went to fire & hell

5 Him who will teach her to be <u>cevel</u>

       her great
It must be friend the divel

    [two lines blank]

Sonnet

O lovely O most charming pug

Thy gracefull air & heavenly mu^g

10 The beauties of his mind do shine

And every bit is shaped so fine

Your very tail is most <u>devine</u>

Your teeth <u>is</u> whiter then the snow

Yor are a great buck & a <u>bow</u>

Your eyes are of so fine a shape

More like a christains then an ape

His cheeks is like the roses blume

Your hair is like the ravens plume

5 His noses cast is of the roman

He is a very pretty weomen

I could not get a ryhme for roman

And was oblidged to call it weoman

[two lines blank]

The Life of the King Jamess

10 At perth poor James the first did die

That wasn't a joy & luxery

And the poor King was murdered ther^e

The nobles to do this did dare

[one line blank]

For he to check their power had tried

This effort made, did hurt their pride

The second James was not so good

To break his promise I knᵒw he would

5 He once did say into an earl

He would not bring him into perl

He bid him come to Stirling castle

In this James behaved like a rascle

Upon the Kings word he relied

10 And to the castle he then hied

wished him
He to give up the confedracy

I would have don't if I was he

The earl refused to do that thing

     quite
At this furious was the King

He put his sword into his guts

And gave him many direfull cuts

5 His vaßals all to arms ran

Their leader was a couardly man

From the feild he ran with terror

       great
I must say this was an error

He was killed by a cannon splinter

10 In the middle of the winter

Perhaps it was not at that time

        me
But I could get no other ryh

James the third was very mean

And with mean persons he was seen

He loved others more then his nobels

That was the cause of all his troubles

Very much he them insulted

5 And he seldom them consulted

For a long time this he had done

At last they got his youthfull son

And in battle he did ingage

Though he was fifteen years of a^{ge}

10 They marched against the very K^{ing}

For having been both bad & mean

James the thirds life ends this way

Of his faults take care I say

James the fourth was a charming prince

15 We have not got a better since

In flodden field alas fell he

The Lords were vexed this to see

Thus fell a good King & a brave

He fell untimely to his grave

James the fifth loved favourites too

Which was a thing he should not do

At Pinkey were his armies killed

And with triump they were not filled

5 He died of grief & of dispair

His nobles for this did not care

Thus fell five Kings most crually

When I hear of them I'm ready to sigh

A King I should not like to be

10 I'd be frightened for a conspiracy

[six lines left blank]

Amend Bone Amend Bon

Amend Bone Amend Bone

Amend Bone Amend Bone

Amend Bone Amend Bone

5 *Amend Bone Amend Bone*

Amend Bone Amend Bone

Amend Bone Amend Bone

Amend Bone Amend Bone

Amend Bone Amend Bone

10 *Amend Bone Amend Bon*^{e}

Amend Bone Amend Bone

Amend Bone Amend Bone

Marjory Fleming Kirkaldy July 19

MARJORY'S LETTERS

LETTER I

[Marjory, in Edinburgh, to her elder sister Isabella : undated]

My dear Isa

I now sit down on

my botom to answer all

your kind and beloved

s letters which you was so

good as to write to me.

This is the first time

I ever wrote a letter

in my Life.—There

are a great many

Girls in the Square

and they cry just

like a pig when we

5 are under the pain

⌐full neceßity of putting

it to Death.—Miss

Potune a Lady of my

acquaintance praises me

10 dreadfully.—I repeated

something out of Deen

Sweft and she said

I was fit for the Stage

and you may think

5 I was primmed up

with majestick Pride

but upon my word I

felt myselfe turn a

little birsay birsay is

10 a word which is a word

that William com⸗

⸗posed which is as you

may suppose a little

enraged.—This horid

5 fat Simpliton says

that my Aunt is

beautifull which is intire

⸗ly impoßible for that

is not her nature.—

LETTER II

[Marjory, presumably in Edinburgh, to her mother: undated, but clearly of 1809. Original now lost: copied by
permission from Macbean (1904), pp. 47-49]

My Dear Mud,

   *I hope you are well : give my love to Isa and Baby, and I will
send them something. I have been often at Ravelstone and once at
Aunt Fleming and Mrs. Miller. I've been acquainted with many*
5 *very genteel girls, and Janetta is a very fine one. Help is been
confined another time. My sleeves is tucked up, and it was very
disagreeable, my collar, and I abhorred it amoniable. I saw the most
prettyist two tame pidgeons you ever saw and two very wee small
kittens like our cat. I am very much acquainted with a young gentle-*
10 *man called Mordecai that I am quite in love with, another called
Captain Bell, and Jamie Keith, and Willie's my great tormentor. A
good-natured girl gave me a song book, and I am very happy. I'll
go down and be thinking when I'm eating my dinner more to tell you,
Mud.*

15 *Aunt has got two of the most beautifullest Turtle Doves you ever
saw. They coo for everlasting and fight. The hawk is in great
spirits, it is a nice beast, the gentlest animal that ever was Seen. Six
canaries, two green linnets, and a Thrush. Isa has been away for a
long time and I've been wearying for her Sadly. I like Isa and Nan*
20 *very much. I play in the back green, and bring in worms for the
thrush. I've done a pair of garters for Isabella but one of them is to*

Short. I will work it larger and work some for Nancy too. I get very long tasks, and when I behave I get them short. Orme Keir is the greatest recovery ever was, and he's thinking about business. My aunt lets out the Birds to get the air in her room. The young gentleman I was speaking of Mordecai, he's very funny. James Keith hardly ever Spoke to me. he said Girl! make less noise, and, when there was a storm sometimes said take out away all your iron, and once before he said, Madgie, go and dance, which I was very proud of. Mind my Dear Mud to return this letter when you return Isabella's. I've forgot to say, but I've four lovers, the other one is Harry Watson, a very delightful boy. Help is very like a tiger when he bites his fleas, a fine, gentle, wise creetyur. Willie was at the Moors, but he soon came back again, for the Moors was like a fish pond like Miss Whyts. I've Slept with Isabella but she cannot Sleep with me. I'm so very restless. I danced over her legs in the morning and she cried Oh dear you mad Girl, Madgie, for she was sleepy. The whole house plagues me about " Come haste to the wedding ", for there is no sense in it ; they think, because it is an Merican, Eliza Purves taught me, they plague me about it exceeding much. I'm affronted to say it, it is so awkward.

Remember your dear Madgie.

Amen.

Finis.

M.F.   Six years old.

LETTER III

[Marjory to her elder sister Isabella: dated 1st April, 1811. Fragmentary.   On the back of it is Isabella Keith's letter to Isabella Fleming, Letter A in the Appendix]

Edinburgh April 1st 1811

My dear Isabella

    I hear that your health has been declining of late I was greatly dißapointed that
5 *you did not come over I should have been so happy to see you I send you an orange I got at General Diroms where I was drinking tea I am studying much at present and I hope improving my mind,—a new cousin of*
10 *mine offered me marriage and his name is Charels Balfour and he is handsome to exceeß*

[the rest is torn off]

LETTER IV

[Marjory to Isabella Keith : dated 26th July, 1811, from Kirkcaldy]

I am now in my native land

And see my dear friends all at hand

There is a thing that I do want

With you the beauteous walks to haun

5 *We would be happy if you would*

Try to come over if you could

Then I would quite happy be

Now & for all eternity

Isa is so very kind

10 *A better girl I could not find*

My mother is so very sweet

And checks my appetite to eat

My father shews us what to do

But I am sure that I want you

I would be happy you to see

For I am sure that I love thee

You are the darling of my heart

With you I cannot bear to part

5 The watter falls we go to see

I am as happy as can be

In pastures sweet we go & stray

I could walk there quite well all day

At night my head on turf could lay

10 There quite well could I sleep all night

The moon would give its tranciant light

I have no more of poetry

O Isa do remember me

And try to love your Marjory

15   Kirkaldy 26th July 1811.

LETTER V

[Marjory to Isabella Keith : dated 1st September, 1811]

My Dear little Mama

I was truly happy to

hear that you are all well.   My

mother bid me tell you that you

5 *are delaying your visit to long*

for you will not get out which

will be a hard restrai^{n}t to you.

We are surrounded with

measles at present on every

10 *side for the Herons got it an^{d}*

Isabella Heron was near

deaths door and one night

her father lifted her out of bed

And she fell down as they thou^ght

lifeleß Mr Heron said that laßie

is dead now she said I'm no dead

yet she then threw up a big

5 worm nine inches and a half

long. My Mother regrets she

cannot write to you at present as her

eyes are very sore. I have begun

dancing but am not very fond

10 of it for the boys strikes and

mocks me. I have been another

night at the dancing & like it

better. I will write to you as often

as I can but I am afraid I shall

15 not be able to write you every. ^week

I long for you with the longings

of a child to embrace you to fold

you in my arms I respect

you with respect due to a mother.

5 *You dont know how I love you*

so I shall remain your loveng

child M Fleming

   Kirkaldy Septr. 1st. 1811

LETTER VI

[Marjory to Isabella Keith : dated 12th October, 1811, from Kirkcaldy]

My Dear Mother

      You will think that I en
-tirely forget you but I aßure
you that you are greatly
5 *mistaken. I think of you all-*
ways and often sight to
think of the distance between
us two loving creatures of nature
We have regular hours for all
10 *ours occupations first at 7 oclock*
we go to the dancing and
come home at 8 we then ~~we~~
read our bible and get our
repeating then we play till 10
15 *then we get our musick till 11*

when we get our writing an

accounts we sew from 12 till 1 &

play till dinner after which

I get my gramer and then

5 work till five at 7 we come & knit *t*

knit till 8 when we dont go to the

dancing this is an exact descrip

⁓tion of our employments.

You have disappointed us all

10 very much especially me in

not coming over every coach

I heard I ran to the window

but I was always disapoint

⁓ed I must take a hasty fare

15 well to her whom I love re⁓

⁓verence & doat on and whom

I hope thinks the same of

Marjory Fleming. P S

An old pack of cards would be

very exeptible

5 *Kircaldy 12 Octr 1811.*

LETTER VII

[Marjory to Isabella Keith, Braehead: undated, but
clearly answered by Isa's letter of November, 1811, Appx. B.
Sent by the hand of Marjory's brother William]

My Dear Isa

*   I wish I was William*

that I might see you. I have

a musick book for the violon

5 *⸌cello and harpsichord and*

a sermon book which I

would have sent to you if my

mother said to ask you

first if you would take it

10 *Tell the Miß Crawfurds*

that I always remember

them Tell the eldest that I

keep the box as a Memento

Mori adieu dear Isa

P S Write the first & last

verse of hill valen again ad^{ieu}

LETTER VIII

[Marjory to Isabella Keith at 1 North Charlotte Street,
Edinburgh: postmarked "No[vember] 1811". Fragmentary]

loving. She is quite sirprised

that she has not hard^e from
any of you on which I will
compose the following poem

5 *O Isa why do not you write*

I'm out of mind when out of ^sight
I am afraid your dead & gone

And thus I do begin my moa^n

O miresable unhappy chi^ld

10 *To lose a mistreß meak & mild*
With all the graces which adorn
I wish that I was never born
I cannot bear the thought O no
Indeed I wish it was not so

15 *Thine eyes with luster will not ^spark*

And in the grave where it is ^dark

Thow shalt be layed a lady fa^r

It fills my hart with great dis-^pair

(a line cut off at foot)

Indeed I now must say adie_u

Both to Isabel and you

LETTER IX

[Marjory's last poem: the original written by her on her slate, Sunday, 15th December, 1811, four days before her death (see Appx. E): the copy preserved is not in Marjory's hand, but was doubtless copied out by Isabella or Elizabeth Fleming]

Addreß to dear Isabella on the Authors
recovery

O Isa pain did visit me
I was at the last extremity
5 *How often did I think of you*
I wished your graceful form to view
To clasp you in my weak embrace
Indeed I thought Id run my race.
Good Care Im sure was of me taken
10 *But indeed I was much shaken*
At last I daily strength did gain
And O at last away went pain
At length the docter thought I might
Stay in the Parlour till the night
15 *I now continue so to do*
Farewell to Nancy and to you.   Wrote by M F.

APPENDIX

Extracts from Letters to and concerning Marjory

LETTER A

[ISABELLA KEITH *to* ISABELLA FLEMING : *1 April 1811. Fragmentary*]

My Dear Isabella

I hope you will excuse the shortness of Maidie's letter and trusting to a longer one from her soon accept of a few lines from me instead,—she is going on very busily with her lessons in all of which she is I hope improving, except her musick she dislikes it so much that she loses all patience, but I hope when she gets the length of playing a Tune she will like it better and pay more attention.—She is very fond of History and is reading the history of Scotland at present in which she is much interested. She continues her journal every day entirely by herself it is a very amusing production indeed, and when finished I shall send it over for your Mothers perusal, and I hope she will find it more correct and better written than the last. I have almost entirely given up her dancing, as it took up a great deal too much time, and a few lessons a year or two after this will do her infinitely more good, she is grown excessively fat and strong, but I cannot say she is in great beauty just now, as she has lost her two front teeth, and her continual propensity to laugh exhibits the defect rather unbecomingly. I have now I think said enough of our dear Muffy, and will talk of other matters. The next great object of our interest is the dear. . . . .

LETTER B

[THE SAME *to* MARJORY FLEMING : [*November 1811*]]

My dear Marjory,

I take the opportunity of your brother Williams going over to write you a few lines, which I hope you will not delay answering. I cannot see that a letter once a week can be a great hardship to you as it might serve instead of your writing Lesson, and you will always find plenty to say if you tell me about your Mother your Sisters and Yourself :—

I am still enjoying this delightful weather at sweet Braehead. Margaret has been rather delicate for a few weeks past, and is not able to take long walks, but Isabella and I go to Barnbougle and the Seaside every day, I very often take my little glass and look over to Kirkaldie, I see Raith Tower perfectly plainly, and I would see Kirkaldie too were it not situated in the bay. This would be very pleasant, for with a telescope I could distinguish the figures on the opposite side of the water and then I might perhaps see you and Isa at play in the fields, only I am afraid I might sometimes be vexed by observing your behaviour to gentle Isa which I am sorry to hear is not exactly what it ought to be do you remember what conversations you and I used to have on this subject ?—and how often you assured me you were sorry for having been cross to Isabella when you were young, and that you were resolved you should always for the future be kind and obedient to her. I hope in your next Letter you will be able to tell me you are trying to be mild and tractable and good humoured.

I long much my dear daughter to see you and talk over all our old stories together, and to hear you read and repeat. I am tiring for my old friend Cesario, and for poor Lear, and wicked Richard :— how is the dear Multiplication Table going on,—are you still as much attached to 9 times 9 as you used to be ?—

I have not Helvellyn here but I think I can remember it by heart pretty correctly :—

I climbed the dark brow of the mighty Helvellyn . . .

[*She proceeds to quote the whole of Scott's poem, ending with Marjory's favourite lines (see p. 120)*]

But meeter for thee gentle Lover of Nature
[To bow] down thy head like the meek Mountain Lamb

When wildered it drops from some cliff huge in sta[ture]
And draws its last sob by the side of its Dam
And more stately thy couch by this desert Lake ly[ing]
Thy obsequies sung by the gray plover flying
With one only friend but to witness thy dying
In the arms of Helvellyn and Catchedicam.

May and Isy Crawfurd send their love and a Kiss to you. I wish I had you by me, and I would give you twenty myself farewell my dear Muff dont forget your Isabella.

I am very much pleased with William's manner, and so were all here ; I regret I saw so little of him, but he has promised to write to me,—

I opened my letter again to say how much I am obliged to you for the off[er of the] Sermons and the Music book. If it is not robbing your Mother or yourself I [would] receive them with great gratitude, and would feel their value encreased in [   ] were you to exercise your wits in writing a line or two of poetry in the [   ] page of each :—

[*Addressed* :]   For

> Miss Muff, Maidie, Marjorie Fleming
> Kirkaldy
> favored by *Rare* Rear Admiral Fleming [1]

LETTER C

[MRS. FLEMING *to* ISABELLA KEITH : *9 January* [1812]]

. . . . Her poor Father unceasingly deplores his loss, I fear he idolised her too much and was too vain of her talents. . . .

To tell you what your poor Maidie said of you would fill volumes, for you was the constant theme of her discourse, the subject of her thoughts, and ruler of her actions—for what would reflect credit or

[1] I.e. William.

reproach on your tuition were the motives by which she was chiefly actuated or restrained, and I loved her the more for the affection she bore you, which was truly filial. The last time she mentioned you was a few hours before all sense save that of suffering was suspended when she said to Dr. Johnstone " If you will let me out at the New Year I will be quite contented." I asked what made her so anxious to get out then : she replied " I wish to purchase a new years gift for Isa : Keith with the Sixpence you gave me for being patient during the Measles, and would like to chuse it myself " I do not recollect her speaking afterwards except to complain of her poor head, till just before she expired when she articulated oh Mother Mother. I send wt this what she esteemed most her Bibles for you and pocket book for Nancy.... [and hair.... Asks for a portrait of Maidie and copies of Burns' "Why am I loth" and the speech of Constance, " Look who comes here. . . ."]

LETTER D

[ISABELLA KEITH to MRS. FLEMING : [after 15 Jan. 1812]]

I have all her writing copies, spelling book, and many other little trifles which I collected after she left me, any of which or even her journals, much as I value all of them, if you wish for them I shall part with but only to her Mother will I ever relinquish the smallest trifle that ever belonged to her. . . .

. . . . the strictness and severity of the mistress which I have often found a painful restraint on my affection. I should have enjoyed her society as a companion and a playmate ; it is foolish and needless to harass myself with such regrets. . . .

I am sorry to see from what he [Mr. Fleming] says, that he anticipates success in my attempt to trace our dear childs features, the sketch I have is a few coarse lines, in which I believe nobody but myself could trace any resemblance, as I never have been in the habit of drawing any finished picture of that kind, the little sketch I shall make, will be of the slightest nature, such as it shall turn out, you shall have it, but I fear my own over anxiety to produce a likeness will, (as I have often found the case) be fatal to my success in the attempt. . . .

LETTER E

[ELIZABETH FLEMING *to* DR. JOHN BROWN, *quoted by him in his essay. Circ. 1863*]

Her birth was 15th January 1803 ; her death 19th December 1811. I take this from her Bibles.[1] I believe she was a child of robust health, of much vigour of body, and beautifully formed arms, and until her last illness, never was an hour in bed. She was niece to Mrs. Keith, residing in No. 1, North Charlotte Street, who was *not* Mrs. Murray Keith, although very intimately acquainted with that old lady. My aunt was a daughter of Mr. James Rae, surgeon, and married the younger son of old Keith of Ravelstone. Corstorphine Hill belonged to my aunt's husband ; and his eldest son, Sir Alexander Keith, succeeded his uncle to both Ravelstone and Dunnottar. The Keiths were not connected by relationship with the Howisons of Braehead, but my grandfather and grandmother (who was), a daughter of Cant of Thurston and Giles-Grange, were on the most intimate footing with *our* Mrs. Keith's grandfather and grandmother ; and so it has been for three generations, and the friendship consummated by my cousin William Keith marrying Isabella Craufurd.

As to my aunt and Scott, they were on a very intimate footing. He asked my aunt to be godmother to his eldest daughter Sophia Charlotte. I had a copy of Miss Edgeworth's *Rosamund, and Harry and Lucy* for long, which was " a gift to Marjorie from Walter Scott,"

---

[1] Her Bible is before me ; *a pair,* as then called ; the faded marks are just as she placed them. There is one at David's lament over Jonathan. [J. B.]

probably the first edition of that attractive series, for it wanted *Frank*, which is always now published as part of the series, under the title of *Early Lessons*. I regret to say these little volumes have disappeared.

Sir Walter was no relation of Marjorie's, but of the Keiths, through the Swintons; and, like Marjorie, he stayed much at Ravelstone in his early days, with his grand-aunt Mrs. Keith; and it was while seeing him there as a boy, that another aunt of mine composed, when he was about fourteen, the lines prognosticating his future fame that Lockhart ascribes in his Life to Mrs. Cockburn, authoress of " The Flowers of the Forest " :

> " Go on, dear youth, the glorious path pursue
>   Which bounteous Nature kindly smooths for you ;
>   Go bid the seeds her hands have sown arise,
>   By timely culture, to their native skies ;
>   Go, and employ the poet's heavenly art,
>   Not merely to delight, but mend the heart."

Mrs. Keir was my aunt's name, another of Dr. Rae's daughters. . . .

I have to ask you to forgive my anxiety in gathering up the fragments of Marjorie's last days, but I have an almost sacred feeling to all that pertains to her. You are quite correct in stating that measles were the cause of her death. My mother was struck by the patient quietness manifested by Marjorie during this illness, unlike her ardent, impulsive nature ; but love and poetic feeling were unquenched. When Dr. Johnstone rewarded her submissiveness with a sixpence, the request speedily followed that she might get out ere New Year's day came. When asked why she was so desirous of getting out, she immediately rejoined, " Oh, I am so anxious to buy something with my sixpence for my dear Isa Keith." Again, when lying very still, her mother asked her if there was anything she wished : " Oh, yes ! if you would just leave the room door open a wee bit, and play ' The Land o' the Leal ', and I will lie and *think*, and enjoy myself" (this is just as stated to me by her mother and mine). Well, the happy day came, alike to parents and child, when Marjorie was allowed to come forth from the nursery to the parlour. It was Sabbath evening, and after tea. My father, who idolised this child, and never afterwards in my hearing mentioned her name, took her in his arms ; and while walking her up and down the room, she said, " Father, I will repeat something to you ; what would you like ? " He said, " Just choose yourself, Maidie." She hesitated for a moment between the paraphrase, " Few are thy days and full of woe," and the lines of Burns already quoted, but decided on the latter, a remarkable choice for a child. The repeating these lines seemed to stir up the depths of feeling in her soul. She asked to be allowed to write a poem ; there was a doubt whether it would be right to allow her, in case of hurting her eyes. She pleaded earnestly, " Just this once ; " the point was yielded, her slate was given her, and with great rapidity she wrote an address of fourteen lines, " to her loved Cousin on the author's recovery," her last work on earth :—

> " Oh ! Isa, pain did visit me . . .
> [etc. as on p. 176.]

She went to bed apparently well, awoke in the middle of the night with the old cry of woe to a mother's heart, " My head, my head ! " Three days of the dire malady, " water in the head," followed, and the end came.

NOTES

PAGE	LINE	
3.	14.	Nettle geranium, an old name of *Coleus fruticosus*, unfamiliar to modern horticulturists.
4.	4.	The only allusion to dolls that Marjory makes.
	10.	*Tales from Fashionable Life*, by Maria Edgeworth, began publication in 1809.
	11.	From 'campels me' to 8, 3 makes one page of Brown's transcript (cf. Macbean's facsimile).
5.	6.	Brown misread this; he transcribes 'as For my cousins', which Macbean naturally prints.
6.	1.	Ossian's poems: the compositions of James Macpherson (1736-1796), partly based on traditional Gaelic legends.
	10.	This was an Exhibition of pictures by Scottish Artists, opened on 9th April, 1810. Cf. 14, 5. For 'and' Brown miscopied 'an', followed by Macbean.
7.	1.	The superscript 'fie' is in Isa Keith's hand: so also pp. 27, 8 and 29, 10.
	3.	'Celadon and his Amelia were a matchless pair'—in Thomson's *Seasons* (Summer: ll. 1171-1222). They walked in the country, and in a thunderstorm Amelia was killed by lightning in Celadon's arms.
	7.	'Mr. Cunhaming': Burns wrote more than one poem to 'Alexander Cunningham, Writer'; probably the one Marjory means is that beginning 'Now spring has clad the groves in green'. 'Writer' does not imply 'Writer to the Signet'.

10-14. 'Fabulous Histories, designed for the Instruction of Children respecting their treatment of animals', by Mrs. Sarah Trimmer, was published 1786; seventh edition, 1802: ultimately the work was entitled the *History of the Robins*; two parent birds and the four offspring here named. Marjory writes 'Peccay' twice, quite clearly, but the original is 'Pecksy'—who 'had no outward charms to recommend her to notice, but they were doubly supplied by the sweetness of her disposition. Her temper was constantly serene; she was ever attentive to the happiness of her parents, and would not have grieved them for the world' (chap. IV).

8.   2. 'Genius Demedicus': doubtless, as Brown suggests, the 'Venus de Medici' (in the Uffizi, Florence).

10.   1. 'musical glasses' (or 'harmonica'): a set of glass plates (tubes, hemispheres, etc.), often supported on a resonance-box, played or struck with the finger or wooden hammer.

      9. 'Tales of the Castle': a series of stories translated by Thomas Holcroft from the Countess de Genlis' *Les Veillées du Château*: Marjory might have seen any of the first three editions. Or possibly 'New Tales of the Castle', further translations from the same source, by Mrs. Mary Pilkington (second edition, 1803).

14.   7. *The Mysteries of Udolpho*, by Mrs. Radcliffe, published 1794, alluded to again on p. 24.

15.   7. 'The Monk and the Vinedresser.' Mr. Michael Sadleir informs me that this is a one-volume work, but he has never been able to trace the authorship.

      13. Who was 'my cousin John'? John Keith, the youngest son of the Ravelston family, is said to have

been deaf and dumb. He is named on p. 37 ; but there are indefinite Johns on pp. 51 and 84.

18.   1.   The birthday of George III was the 4th of June, which in 1810, his jubilee year, was widely celebrated. This allusion is one of the dating-points for this Journal.

19.   10.   This curious idea Marjory repeats, p. 30, l. 9, perhaps owing to inability to find another rhyme.

21.   4.   'Wed away' (*i.e.* weeded out) : clearly an allusion to the ancient refrain to an ancient Scottish air :
> ' The Flowers of the Forest are a' wede away '

to which Jean Elliot wrote her well-known poem :
> ' I've heard them lilting at our ewe-milking ',

and Alicia Cockburn hers :
> ' I've seen the smiling
> Of fortune beguiling ',

both of which were composed about 1765.

22.   6.   The two periods are perhaps Marjory's attempt at an apostrophe : lessons in punctuation came later. (See p. 60).

23.   7.   Brown printed :
'And with great care within I creep'.

24.   9.   Brown printed 'fighting' for 'figiting', and took other liberties with this passage.

26.   1.   Possibly Mr. Philip 'Caddle': see 77, 9.

28.   1.   The top line appears to be a model for copying, doubtless written by Isa Keith ; the capital N in particular is too good to be Marjory's.

29.   1.   Farnie omitted the last three lines of this famous poem : Brown's version also omits ll. 6-7 and 10-11. Both conceal the fact that Marjory's best-known couplet (ll. 14, 15) is really part of a triplet.

11. 'pows': unmistakably so written by Marjory: Macbean printed 'fows'. Almost certainly Marjory meant to write 'powts' or 'pouts', the Scottish form of 'poult', which is 'in vulgar language applied to the chicken of any domesticated fowl' (Jamieson's *Dictionary*). If she had not heard it in the Braehead farmyard, she might have read it in Burns (*Epistle to John Rankine*):

'And the wee pouts begin to cry.'

31.   1. 'Giffords Fair': Gifford is a small town in Haddingtonshire at the foot of the Lammermuir Hills. The fairs were held in March, June and October, so the allusion scarcely helps to date the entry.

34.   14. 'the fasts by good Nelson': *Companion for the Festivals and Fasts of the Church of England,* by Robert Nelson, 1704: a very popular manual, of which innumerable editions were issued for over a century.

JOURNAL II

37.   1. Above Marjory's first line, in Isa Keith's hand is written 'Braehead'.

        6. The correction 'are' interlined is one of the very few in Isa Keith's hand: there are others on the next page, in lines 3 and 9.

38.   1. 'Crakyhall', Craigiehall, now a hotel-club. In Marjory's time it belonged to the Hope Veres of Blackwood, but may have been let.

39.   3. Ravelston, the Keiths' home.

40.   1-4. These entries are in Isa Keith's hand, written in before Marjory came to this page; each begins with the word 'Marjory', and presumably records her doings—

or misdoings—for the days mentioned ; but they have been almost completely obliterated. If they could be deciphered, something significant might emerge ; at least we have the date ' Thursday July 12th ', which of the possible years fits 1810 only, and provides a valuable dating-point.

42.   3.   After ' whip ' the paper is torn, and apparently ' ss ' has been written in above.

     11.   ' Tuesday 4 ' may refer to September, 1810. The note, in Isa Keith's hand, appears to be quite casual, and was clearly there before Marjory set ' hir ' beside it.

43-44.   This leaf lacks about an inch and a half at the bottom, obviously removed before Marjory wrote, as her text is continuous from 43 to 44, and 44, 10 is squeezed in, and in the absence of ruled lines curves up and down.

47-48.   The lower portion, four inches, of this leaf is cut away. But immediately below ' cant ' (47, 5) appears the top of another word, proving that a passage has been excised. On p. 48, however, Marjory has adapted her writing to the cut leaf.

48.   3.   Notable as the only place where Marjory spells Braehead correctly, out of a dozen attempts.

51.   11.   ' sina ' : senna.

54.   10.   This passage is quoted by Brown about Braehead instead of Ravelston.

     11.   ' balm wine ' : a herbal distillation. Scott's *Antiquary* rudely calls it an ' infernal decoction ' (chap. VI).

55.   2, 3.   Brown prints ' the delight of my soul '.

56.   12.   Under ' Mordica ' there is a scribble, deleted.

60.   1-4.   Marjory's enthusiasm for ' simecolings ' and ' commoes ' may be observed hereabouts: 57, 6 ; 58, 8 ; 59, 6 ; and at the foot of this page.

62. 1. I have failed to discover the source of this classical story.

67. 9. Macbean prints 'larkies', which may be Brown's misreading.

73-74. This leaf is defective both at top and bottom, but it is at the top that the greater portion is missing—perhaps the result of the 'passion'?

73. 8. In the last three lines of this page Marjory's handwriting rapidly degenerates, as though the 'dreadful passion' were still shaking her.

     10. 'lick': the schoolboy's term was known to Marjory, it seems.

77. 9. 'Caddle': doubtless a Cadell of Cramond (see note on 110, 8).

78. 6. '2 3' represents 'two-three', not twenty-three.

88. 4. The interlined words are in Isa Keith's writing.

     5. This word, beautifully written, is clearly Isa Keith's 'copy' for her pupil. Marjory's first two attempts leave out the *a*; later she leaves out an *m* or two.

89. 1. This line is also obviously a model set by Isa Keith.

91. 9. Isabella Craufurd afterwards married William Keith, Isa's brother and one of Marjory's 'three well made Bucks' (p. 37): a Ravelston-Braehead marriage. Burke's *Landed Gentry* gives the date of the marriage as 1844, incredibly late. See Appx. E.

     10. 'Baron bugal', Barnbougle Castle, on the shores of the Firth of Forth: a walk of about two miles from Braehead, through Dalmeny Park.

92. 15. 'Lot and his wife' were reported by Brown as still thriving in 1863. Mr. Esdaile in 1930 saw yews in the garden, but could not identify this particular pair.

JOURNAL III

95-96.   The inner bottom corner of this, the outside leaf of the Journal, is torn away.

95. 9, 10.   This offer of marriage affords a dating-point, as Marjory relates it to her sister Isabella in Letter III (p. 163), which is dated April 1st, 1811.

11-14.   The first two hiatus are easily emended, the second two must be conjectured. Brown misread 'plainly' as 'plenty' and prints 'nay plenty heard me': Macbean more reasonably emends 'nay plainly [love]d me'. In 14 he suggests 'to the wicked' for the torn portion, but there is not room enough.

96.   7.   'Cosin': Marjory wrote 'sosin', then altered the first letter to a C.

11-14.   The ends of the lines are torn, and Marjory obviously was muddled. Macbean prints 'many people have su[pped] in mesery & have not had fortitude & [courage] to suppress there ——'.

97.   I think these two words are undoubtedly written by Marjory, though probably at Isa Keith's orders.

Macbean is misled at this point, owing to having only Brown's copy before him, which gives a whole page to the words 'Careless Marjory', while the opposite page covers our pages 96 (foot) to 100 (top). Macbean comments that the 'careless' refers to Marjory's misspellings on 99, whereas it was clearly intended to rebuke the corrections and errors on 96.

98.   1.   Brown omitted 'is': Macbean restored it.

2.   The allusion might conceivably be to *Observations upon the Prophecies* by the famous Sir Isaac Newton, published in 1733, as Macbean suggests, but is much

more probably to the *Dissertation on the Prophecies* by Thomas Newton, Bishop of Bristol, 3 vols., 1754-8, of which there was a tenth edition in 1804.

3-4. For the deletion Macbean suggests '[I wonder if]'.

10. 'Miss Potune' occurs again in Marjory's Letter I (p. 157) as the 'Simpliton': she is 'fat' in both places. The name is quite clearly written: Brown printed 'Portune'. 'Fortune' is possible.

99. 10-14. The bottom corner was torn, even when Brown made his copy, but the restoration of the missing letters is easy.

100. 11. '*Self-control*', by Mary (Balfour) Brunton, whose husband was a minister in Edinburgh from 1803, was published anonymously in 1811, and the first edition sold out in a month. This allusion is therefore a useful dating-point. The *Scots Magazine* for 1811 announces the book in February, reviews it at great length in March, and announces the second edition in May.

102. 1. Above this line appears, in a hand certainly adult, but not (as Macbean suggests) Isa Keith's, the statement 'composed & written at the age of six years'. Unless the poem was written when Marjory was six, *i.e.* in 1809, and copied in here later, it would appear to be impossibly at variance with the other indications of date.

'Ephibol': '(epigram or epitaph—who knows which ?),' is Brown's comment; 'epitaph or eulogium,' Macbean's. The word is some 'portmanteau' of two or more words confused by Marjory; possibly 'epistle' is one ingredient.

10-13. Brown omitted these lines.

103. 13. 'maxium' or 'maxuim': there is no dot to the *i*.

14. Marjory did not write in the final word, clearly 'ever'.

104. 1-6. Marjory names three of Maria Edgeworth's popular
       Tales: 'Lazy Lawrence', 'Tarlton', and 'The
       False Key'.

105.   1. John Bannister, a London comedian long famous at
       Drury Lane and mentioned by Charles Lamb,
       produced a one-man entertainment of songs, etc.,
       which he called 'Bannister's Budget', and toured it
       with great success all over England during 1808. In
       March 1809 he was in Glasgow and Edinburgh; in
       the latter he gave the 'Budget' in the George Street
       Assembly Rooms (cf. Adolphus, *Memoirs of John
       Bannister*, 1839, ii. chap. 27.). There are difficulties in
       attributing this Journal to 1809; but as the 'Budget'
       was a great success, it is probable that a return visit was
       paid in the following years. I have however failed
       to trace any record in 1811.

109. 1-2. The lacunae are tantalising. Who 'is one of our
       beauties'?

      13. A definite dating-point. 'General Grame' is Sir
       Thomas Graham (afterwards Lord Lynedoch), who
       'defeated the French' notably at Barossa (or Barrosa),
       5th March, 1811. A London Gazette Extraordinary
       of March 25th printed his despatch of the 6th, and
       the event was chronicled in the *Scots Magazine* for
       March. It must be this famous victory which reached
       Marjory's ears. A vote of thanks to Graham was
       passed by the House of Commons on March 28th.

110.   1. Another tantalising loss: what was the 'tumbling
       ——' that the French prisoners made?

       2. Enough remains round the obliteration at the end of
       the line to support my reading. Macbean, from
       Brown's copy, prints 'made ccips (? slips)'.

       8. Another significant dating-point. 'Macary' was

James McArra, tried on 21st January, 1811, and convicted of the murder of his brother (both 'in liquor' at the time). He was sentenced on Feb. 20th to banishment for life. He was an 'iron slitter' in the works of Cadell and Company of Cramond: which may suggest a reason for Marjory's hearing of the case (see Philip 'Caddle', p. 77). But it was sensational enough to be reported at length in the *Scots Magazine*, 1811, pp. 153-5.

113.   6.   The Newgate Calendar has ceased to be 'Amusing', as it was on p. 107.

13.   'riveluts': Macbean, from Brown's copy, prints 'revelats', which Marjory's corrected word cannot support. I think she finally got the right letters in the wrong order.

114.   8.   *The Pigeon*, as we learn two pages further on, is a tale of Kotzebue's. Marjory may have read it in *Novellettes* by Augustus von Kotzebue, 3 vols., 1807.

115.   8.   'a tile in time'. I can find no explanation for this variation of the old proverb: Hislop's *Scottish Proverbs* gives 'A steek in time saves nine'. Marjory certainly wrote 'tile' quite unmistakably.

9-13.   'Tawny': Macbean, from Brown's copy, 'Fawny'. The 'Cheap Repository' was the general title of a long series of small books (1797-1800), many signed 'Z.', *i.e.* Hannah More: they were sold at 'One Penny or 6s. 6d. per Hundred—Great allowance will be made to Shopkeepers and Hawkers'. The two named are *Tawney Rachel, or the Fortune-teller* and *The Cottage Cook, or Mrs. Jones's Cheap Dishes*: the moral of the first perhaps inspired Marjory's remarks on 'Superstition' (p. 11): the second ends 'Pay your debts, serve God, and love your neighbour'.

119.   6.   Lord Rosebery's 'estate' is Dalmeny Park, hard by Braehead and familiar to Marjory.

120.   3⁄10.   Scott's original verse is partly given in Isa Keith's letter, Appx. B (pp. 180⁄1).

122.   10.   'Moreheads': Robert Morehead's *Series of Discourses upon the Principles of Religious Belief,* second edition, 1809⁄16.

123.   4⁄7.   Another and most regrettable excision: on which side of the leaf was Marjory's indiscretion? Here there appears to have been a record of an escape of prisoners of war from Edinburgh Castle, almost certainly that of April 11, 1811, when nearly fifty men escaped by cutting a hole through the bottom of the parapet wall (possibly Marjory's 'foundation of the barracks') and letting themselves down by a rope. One was killed by a fall. The rest escaped in various directions, and doubtless many in Edinburgh and its environs besides Marjory were afraid of being 'saccrified to death.' However all the escapers were recaptured in due course. The episode clearly provided Stevenson with material for the escape in *St. Ives,* though he dates that story two years later. (*Scots Magazine,* 1811, p. 397: Francis Abell, *Prisoners of War in Britain 1756⁄1815,* p. 273).

126.   11.   'exer': Marjory seems to have been troubled at the letter *v*: in 113, 4 she has written 'exel' for 'evel'; and in 114, 11 'yery' for 'very'.

130.   13.   See note on 110, 8.

131.   3.   'Sanaford': Marjory has omitted the ascender⁄stroke of the first *d.* Daniel Sandford (1766⁄1830) was made Bishop of Edinburgh in 1806. Mr. James is unidentified.

132.   is blank in the original.

Poems appended to Journal I

139-140. The foot of the leaf is cut, but apparently no verses have been lost.

144. 6. Above the words 'Sunday night', which are underlined, a hand, apparently Isa Keith's, has written a word that looks like 'well'.

147. 16. Brown prints: 'I suppose she has gained . . .'

148. 7. Brown's version of this poem contains at least eleven errors in the fourteen lines. In the first, he prints: 'O lively . . .'

      12. Brown omits this line.

      14. Brown prints:
'Your a great buck, your a great beau'.

149. 3. Brown prints: 'Your cheek'.

      8. Brown prints:
'So was obliged to call him woman'.

153. Eight blank pages follow here in the MS.

154. This page seems to be all in Marjory's hand. As it is signed at the foot from Kirkcaldy, it may have been written as a spontaneous exercise.

Marjory's Letters

158. 2. 'the Square': Charlotte Square.

      8. 'Miss Potune': see note on 98, 10.

159. 9. 'birsay' is scarcely 'a word that William composed'; it is ancient Scots for 'bristling', i.e. angered, enraged.

161. It is deeply to be regretted that the original of this letter is now untraceable: Macbean, who must have seen it, as his version is fuller than Brown's, definitely states that it 'was written early in 1809, just after she had

reached six years of age, a fact which she proudly chronicles'. It is thus earlier than any date assignable to the Journals. Many of the names mentioned by Marjory occur nowhere else in her writings: Mrs. Miller, Janetta, Mordecai, Captain Bell, Orme Keir, Harry Watson, Miss Whyte (?), and Eliza Purves; also 'Help'.

In the absence of the original, I have followed Marjory's usual epistolary style and eliminated the paragraphing given to it by Macbean. But there is a distinct break at dinner-time after l. 14.

161. 4. 'Aunt Fleming': doubtless the wife of the Rev. Thomas Fleming, minister of Lady Yester's.

15. 'Aunt': Mrs. Keith.

162. 2. 'Orme Keir': her cousin, son of her mother's sister Elizabeth.

3. For 'recovery' Brown prints 'enemy'.

5. 'Mordecai': this second mention of a young gentle-man 'that I am quite in love with' and who is 'very funny' recalls Journal II, where (pp. 37-8) Marjory says the same two things of Mr. 'Geo. Crakey'. Mordecai is an odd but not unknown name. But Marjory knew the Book of Esther (p. 56), and possibly Mr. Craigie was called 'Geordie Craigie': if she heard his surname as 'Crakey', might she not have heard his whole name as 'Mordecai' at an earlier meeting?

11. 'Harry Watson': Brown notes, 'the venerable founder of the Fine Arts Chair in our University' He died 27 July, 1879.

17. 'Come haste to the Wedding': a song so named was an item in a 'Pantomime called the Elopement' which existed at least as early as 1768 and was current

in one form or another for at least a century thereafter. It is curious to note that another song, 'Come on, jolly lads', from the same Pantomime was 'sung by Mr. Bannister', whose 'Budget' was performed in Edinburgh in the year of this letter (see note p. 105).

163.   7.   'General Diroms': Lt.-Gen. Alexander Dirom, 1757-1830.

          11.   The fragment ends here, but luckily preserves the allusion to Charles Balfour which helps to date Journal III (p. 95).

164.   Marjory is at home: see her dated signature, p. 154.

167.   15.   'write you every week': see Isa's reply in the first paragraph of Appx. B.

173.   1, 2.   Isa in her reply (Appx. B.) writes out the whole poem from memory 'pretty correctly'.

INDEX TO JOURNALS, LETTERS AND VERSES

An INDEX OF THE FIRST LINES of all Marjory's verses will be found at the end of the entry under her name, 'Fleming, Marjory', and her references to literature under 'Books, Poems, and their Authors'.